COLLINS

Practical

GARDENING

SUE PHILLIPS

HarperCollins*Publishers*
London

HarperCollins*Publishers*
London

First published in 2000 by HarperCollins*Publishers*

Most of the text and illustrations in this book were previously
published in the *Collins Complete Garden Manual*

Design and layout © HarperCollins*Publishers* 1999
Text: © Sue Phillips 1999

A catalogue record for this book is available
from the British Library.

ISBN 0-00-414104-0

Designed and produced for HarperCollins*Publishers* by
Cooling Brown, Middlesex, England
Editorial: Carole McGlynn, Ann Kay
Design: Alistair Plumb, Tish Mills, Elaine Hewson
Photography: Peter Anderson, Steve Gorton, Matthew Ward

Colour origination: Colourscan

Printed and bound in Great Britain by Scotprint

The HarperCollins website address is:
www.fireandwater.com

Contents

INTRODUCTION

❖

GARDENERS ARE NOT BORN with green fingers; they acquire them gradually – usually almost without realising it. And it used to be a very slow process.

When I began gardening, at the age of four, most young people got a good grounding by helping their parents and grandparents. You would learn how to weed, dig, plant, dead-head and even mow the lawn, so that by the time you had a house of your own you knew where to start 'doing something' with the space around it.

The perception then was that over many years of practical hands-on experience – learning from your mistakes, sharing experiences with other gardeners, and getting ideas by visiting other gardens – you would hone your skills so that by the time you retired, you would be ready to take up gardening seriously and devote yourself to making a truly magnificent garden.

Thankfully it doesn't happen like that any more – you don't need to spend a lifetime learning the ropes. Today, we want the garden of our dreams NOW, and we'll learn how to look after it along the way. Fortunately, modern gardening techniques and equipment mean that anyone can have a garden that is colourful, comfortable to sit in and easily run. Young, mobile people can create stylish mini gardens that can be virtually picked up and taken with them when they move house. Families are able to create safe gardens that are like outdoor living rooms in which to relax, entertain family and friends and where children can play. Retired or leisured people can have attractive, interesting but easily run gardens that leave them time for other interests too.

Gone is the concept of spending years making a garden that, once finished, stays looking the same for ever. In today's flexible garden we can put in new features, or give an

◁ MODERN GARDEN PRODUCTS, tools, techniques and even plants are all geared to making gardening quicker, easier and more successful than ever before.

4

◁ WITH A KNOWLEDGE OF GARDEN BASICS, *it is possible to create colourful effects all year round, even in a small town garden.*

entire area a fashionable makeover, whenever we fancy a change of scene. New plants are constantly coming along and both gardening magazines and television programmes continue to fire us with enthusiasm. Gardening has never been more alive.

However, because we now put the creative cart before the horticultural horse, while it's easy to make an instant garden that looks wonderful when it is finished, you may not feel quite sure how to look after it. Now that gardening is being ever-simplified, people who have got past that first complete beginner's stage are asking, 'Why do we do this?' or 'What happens if we try it this way?'

This book has been created to fill the gap between creating a lovely garden and keeping it that way. It tells you all you need to know to get the job done and answers the questions you want to ask without overwhelming you with technicalities. You can read it from cover to cover as a crash course in gardening basics, or use it to look up something just before you need to do it. Whether it's pruning or laying a new lawn, it's full of all the things your grandparents would have told you – if only they hadn't already cottoned on to the benefits of today's way of life and taken off on their travels instead.

5

J. Phillips

SUE PHILLIPS

Knowing your soil

Soil is the raw ingredient of gardening, but soils vary greatly in both type and fertility. If the soil is of good quality – deep and fertile – plants virtually grow themselves, but if it is out of condition you will have to improve its structure and its fertility before growing anything in it. So look for a few basic clues to your soil type and its state of health before embarking on planting.

SOIL TEXTURE

There are three main soil types – sandy, clay and loam – and it is important to know which type you have. Assessing the texture of your soil will give the best clues. Since the soil's texture depends on the kind of rock from which its particles were originally formed, you will never be able to change the basic type but there are ways in which you can improve and condition it. Most garden soils are in fact a mixture of several types, and the soil can vary quite considerably, even within the same garden.

Sandy soil feels gritty when rubbed between your hands and the particles do not stick together. Water runs away quickly after rain: you will see that any puddles vanish fast. Sandy soil is light, easily dug and warms up quickly after winter. It drains well but its composition also means that valuable nutrients leach out quickly. It therefore needs the frequent addition of huge amounts of organic matter in some form, such as well-rotted garden compost, which decomposes very quickly in this sort of soil.

◁ **CLAY SOILS** *are heavy to work but can be rough-dug in winter to allow frost to break them down.*

Clay soil is sticky when wet, and puddles last a long time after rain. When dry, clay soil becomes very hard and often cracks badly. Because it compacts into a dense, airless soil, it is heavy to dig but it holds water and therefore nutrients well, although it is prone to waterlogging. Clay soils need the addition of well-rotted organic matter too, but they should also have gritty sand or fine bark chippings dug in to improve their drainage and help aerate them, which makes them easier to work. Because clay has a naturally small particle size, the soil texture needs 'opening up' so that roots can penetrate and plants thrive in it. Heavy blue or yellow clay subsoils should not be dug, to avoid mixing the infertile lower layer with better soil above – simply pile on deep mulches to improve the soil.

Loam is easily recognizable as good garden soil; when cultivated and raked it breaks down to a crumb-like finish. It is rich, retains water without getting waterlogged and plants grow well in it.

Especially if it is dark in colour, loam may need very little improvement, although it is good practice to add organic matter to help maintain its fertility.

SOIL FERTILITY

The gardener's aim is to have a well-balanced, fertile soil but it often takes time and effort to achieve this, especially if you inherit a new plot in which the soil is compacted and full of builder's rubble. But all soils benefit from mixing in some form of organic material, such as compost, which improves both the soil's texture and its fertility.

THE SOIL'S pH VALUE

❖

4.5 or less: Very acid. Rhododendrons, heather and other ericaceous plants grow best.

4.5–5.5: Acid. Ericaceous plants will grow here but liming makes the ground suitable for a wider range of plants.

5.5–6.5: Slightly acid to nearly neutral; a majority of garden plants will thrive.

7.00: Neutral (the pH of pure water).

8.00: Chalk or limestone soil; only lime-lovers are happy here.

◁ **SOIL THAT IS** *kept in good heart by correct cultivation will produce heavy crops of fruit, flowers and vegetables year after year.*

▷ **RHODODENDRONS** *are happiest in acid soil, so check your soil's pH level before growing them to ensure they will thrive.*

It is possible to get a rough idea of whether your soil is very acid or alkaline by observing the plants that grow happily in it. If, for example, rhododendrons or other acid-lovers like camellias, skimmias, heathers or pieris, grow well in neighbouring gardens, it is reasonable to guess that the local soil is acid. Chalky rocks at the side of the road or chalk-loving plants such as pinks, potentillas and cistus growing wild suggests chalky soil. Since the soil's pH determines which plants will grow well in it, it is always worth doing a pH test to check your soil's acidity. Small, inexpensive kits are available in garden centres to do this. Extremely acid soil can be neutralized by using lime, if necessary, while limy soil can be neutralized with sulphur chips and plenty of organic matter, which is usually slightly acidic in reaction. However, the best solution is always to choose appropriate plants for an acid or a chalky soil.

7

Humus is decomposed plant material, broken down by the action of bacteria and other soil organisms like earthworms. It is a natural soil improver and source of nutrients. Worms play an important role in improving soil by making burrows which help aeration and drainage, and by digesting organic matter to make humus and release trace elements. The best way to encourage worms is to add plenty of organic matter to the soil.

The colour of soil will give you clues as to its condition and fertility. A dark colour is an indication that soil has previously been well cultivated and contains plenty of humus. Very light coloured soil often suggests a large proportion of sand or chalk, both of which make a soil dry out fast. Yellow or blue lumps or layers, found below the soil surface, are a sign of badly drained, infertile, heavy clay subsoil.

SOIL ACIDITY

Soil can also vary in its degree of acidity or alkalinity, often referred to as its pH.

USING A SOIL TEST KIT

Take several soil samples from all round the garden, using a trowel to remove a 'core' of soil. Take only soil from below the top 5cm (2in) for the test and avoid areas that have been used for bonfires or mixing cement. Mix all the samples together well or, if the soil is obviously different in some areas, make several separate tests. Follow the manufacturer's instructions on the kit. The usual procedure is to fill the tube with soil from the sample up to a given mark, then add distilled water to the level of the next mark. A chemical is then added, the sample shaken well and the pH determined by comparing the colour of the mix to those on the test card.

Digging and improving your soil

Organic matter is the lifeline of the garden and you should add it at every opportunity for good soil structure and fertility. Dig it in deeply by double digging when you first prepare a new bed, fork more in when getting annual beds ready for planting, and spread it over the ground as a mulch in permanent shrub, rose, perennial and mixed borders.

ORGANIC MATTER

Bulky organic matter can take several forms, all of which improve soil structure by creating air spaces between the fine mineral particles that make up the soil. More air spaces mean better drainage and aeration, which in turn improve growing conditions for plants by making it easier for their roots to penetrate. It also encourages worms, whose activities condition the soil.

Organic matter is primarily a soil conditioner; it supplies only a small amount of nutrients, the most important of which are the trace elements needed in only minute amounts and rarely provided by chemical (or inorganic) fertilizer. For this reason you should add

8

△ **SOW GREEN MANURE** *crops as a carpet under tall plants like sweetcorn. Once the main crop is harvested, dig in the green manure.*

both organic matter and fertilizer to bring the soil to the state of fertility needed for the intensive cultivation required from gardening.

COMPOST AND MANURES

Since you will need organic matter in large amounts, it makes sense to use whatever is available locally, most conveniently and cheaply. Choose from manure, spent hops or old mushroom compost, all of which can be bought in bags from a garden centre if you do not have a local source. You can also recycle used growing bags, or make your own garden compost by recycling garden and household waste via a compost bin: anything organic will serve the purpose

so long as it is well rotted before use. During the stages of its decomposition, plant material is attacked by soil bacteria and nitrogen is consumed in the process; therefore, if 'fresh' materials are dug into the garden, this will result in a nitrogen shortage.

GREEN MANURES

Green manure crops are deliberately sown in order to be dug in; their role is to improve the soil by providing both nutrients and organic matter. Green manure crops, which include clover, buckwheat and grazing rye, are sown like a carpet covering the ground and normally dug in before they flower. Different crops can be used for long- or short-term cover, and for summer or winter use. Long-term green manure crops are a good way of occupying vacant land so that improvement is

△ **TO IMPROVE** *the texture and drainage of heavy clay soils, dig in coarse, sharp sand or fine grit at 1–2 bucketfuls or more per sq m.*

SOIL CARE TOOL KIT

❖

The basic soil care tools are a spade and a digging fork. It is often easier to dig heavy soil with a fork; a fork is also best for spreading compost or manure when improving the soil. But it is better to use a spade on light soil, which would trickle through the tines of a fork. Long-handled spades make the job of digging less of a strain, particularly for people liable to backache.

△ **ADDING LIME** *to acid soil prevents minerals being chemically 'locked up' in the soil.*

taking place in 'down' time. Short-term crops are a way of storing nutrients in the soil during winter, when they may otherwise be leached out by rain, and of returning them to the ground when dug in. Dig green manure crops into the soil six weeks before sowing or planting.

ORGANIC MULCHES

Another way of adding organic matter to the soil is by spreading a layer on top as a mulch. After the initial soil preparation has been done and the beds planted with shrubs or perennials, this is in fact the only way of adding organic material to the soil. A mulch is a layer of material, organic or otherwise, covering the soil. It works by keeping germinated weed seeds and seedlings in the dark, preventing them from growing; it has little effect on established perennial weeds. Suitable mulching materials include well-rotted garden compost or manure, spent mushroom compost, cocoa shell or bark chippings. These are spread annually in a layer 2.5cm (1in) or 5cm (2in) thick over the soil between plants when the soil is moist and weed-free. The mulch is slowly drawn into the soil by the action of worms and will need to be 'topped up' annually. Spring is the usual time but on

light soil it is best to apply a mulch in both spring and autumn.

DEEP BEDS AND RAISED BEDS

Deep beds are narrow, deeply prepared beds used for the intensive cultivation of vegetables. After digging and incorporating quantities of organic matter, the beds are never walked on so the soil does not get compacted. These enriched beds are

worked on from paths alongside them and crops planted closer than usual to produce higher yields. Extra organic matter is spread on top or lightly forked in. Raised beds, used in low-maintenance gardens or to provide better drainage for alpine plants, works in the same way, using a 'no dig' technique after initial deep preparation and improving the soil by spreading organic mulches on top.

DIGGING THE SOIL

❖

1 Divide your plot in half lengthwise and dig a trench the depth and width of your spade, running halfway across one end. Remove soil and pile it up outside the plot.

2 Spread a 5cm (2in) layer of organic matter in the bottom of the trench. Working backwards, dig along the edge of the trench, turning the soil over into it as you work. This fills the first trench with soil, creating a second trench alongside it.

3 Continue to dig and add organic matter, creating successive trenches. When you reach the end of the plot, work your way back up the other side. Fill in the last trench with soil removed from the first.

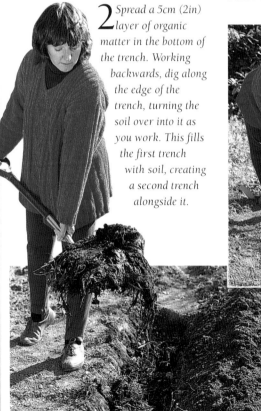

4 For double digging, make the trench the width of two spades. Dig organic matter into the base using a fork, breaking up the soil to the full depth of its prongs. Continue digging down the plot, turning the soil into successive double-width trenches. Use soil removed from the last trench to fill the first.

9

Making compost

Home-made garden compost is easy to make using a variety of waste materials from the kitchen and garden. By recycling your garden waste you can cheaply create a useful form of organic matter to improve soils and mulch borders. Composting also reduces the amount of material being thrown away and pointlessly taking up room in landfill sites.

△ **A COMPOST BIN**
is the ideal domestic recycler, turning kitchen peelings, garden weeds, lawn clippings and other soft, natural waste into free soil-improver.

▷ **NEW MATERIAL**
should be added in layers 15cm (6in) deep, each capped with fresh soil or fresh manure to make it work properly; top the finished heap with a layer of soil.

10

MAKING LEAFMOULD

❖

Autumn leaves, especially oak, take longer to break down than normal compost ingredients – usually a year or more. Small quantities of leaves can be added to a compost heap, mixed in with plenty of soft materials, but large amounts are best composted separately in a leafmould cage, made by tacking wire netting round four corner posts. Each time leaves are gathered up, tip them into the cage, spread them out, dampen and cover with soil. When well-rotted, leafmould is valuable for creating special beds for choice woodland plants, topdressing woodland borders or using as a mulch.

THE SECRETS OF SUCCESS

All manner of soft waste can be used to make compost, including fruit and vegetable peelings from the kitchen. Suitable material from the garden includes weeds, old bedding plants and the leafy debris removed when clearing flower beds; in addition soft hedge clippings and lawn mowings can be composted. For best results, use a mixture of materials – too much of one ingredient can make the heap slimy, especially if very soft, green materials like grass clippings are used.

To speed up the rotting process, add compost ingredients in 15cm (6in) layers, dampening the material if dry, before capping with a bucketful of garden soil or animal manure (fresh, unrotted manure makes a good compost 'starter'), which provides vital bacteria to encourage the heap to rot. Alternatively, sprinkle with a handful of sulphate of ammonia (to provide nitrogen) or a compost activator product.

Continue adding to the heap in this way until the container is full, then finish with a layer of soil. Once a heap is

completed, do not add any further material as this will simply delay the rotting process. Start a second heap instead, if you have space. Two or more compost heaps are needed for peak efficiency, so that one is rotting down while another is being filled.

COMPOST BINS

For small quantities of waste, a compost bin is the answer. Various models are available in garden centres: they resemble plastic dustbins without bases and, by containing the compost, encourage it to

△ A WELL-MADE, FREESTANDING COMPOST HEAP *should take 6–12 months to rot down sufficiently that the compost is ready to use; it will need turning sides-to-middle halfway through.*

heat up quickly and evenly. Since they have solid sides and a lid, material is composted evenly through the bin, so that material round the edges breaks down properly too – there should be no need to 'turn' the heap halfway through the composting time.

COMPOST HEAPS
With bigger gardens that generate large quantities of compostible waste, an open compost heap is the most economical method. Make a container of loose wooden slats, or of wire mesh

◁ A MULCH OF *well-rotted compost, 2.5–5cm (1–2in) thick, covers the soil around plants to retain moisture and smother weeds.*

supported by four corner posts, or even a loose heap of material. In order to work, this will need to be big: at least a 1m (3ft) cube. Being open-sided, the heat will be concentrated in the middle, so turn the heap after three months in order that material from the sides takes a turn in the centre, where it can be composted. Ideally, you should cover a compost heap with plastic sheeting in winter or rainy weather to keep the heat in and excess water out.

WORM BINS
Worm-worked compost is pure wormcast and very rich. It is made using special bins like dustbins with a tap in the base. A breeding colony of tiger worms or brandling worms (available from organic gardening supply firms or from fishing tackle and

COMPOST MATERIAL TO AVOID

- Never put perennial weeds or diseased plant material onto a compost heap, as the heat generated inside it may not be enough to kill the organisms, and you risk spreading them when the compost is later used round the garden.

- Avoid woody material like prunings or the stems of herbaceous plants – these will compost down in time but they take longer than other compost ingredients, thus occupying the heap for longer. If woody materials cannot be disposed of by other means, chop them into short lengths or put them through a mechanical shredder, which will shorten the rotting time, and if possible compost them separately.

- Lawn mowings from grass treated with chemical weedkillers should be kept apart from other compost ingredients for up to six mowings after treatment, and composted separately for at least six months. Use for non-edible plants.

pet shops in summer) is introduced to a layer of pre-rotted material in the base of the bin. Small amounts of finely chopped, soft material like household peelings and similar scraps are then added every few days, to keep the worms 'fed'. Fluid that accumulates in the bin is drained off regularly via the tap, and diluted to use as a plant food. When full of soil-like material, the worms are sieved out to start a new bin. Worm bins need care in setting up and they are tricky to manage until you get used to them, so follow the maker's instructions with your bin.

Watering your garden

Plants are made up of over 90 per cent water, which is taken in through their roots and lost through their leaves by transpiration. When short of water, the plant's natural processes cannot take place properly and their growth suffers; plants may wilt or even die. But nowadays water meters, dry summers and hosepipe bans mean that we must use water wisely and deliver it precisely where it is needed, without using wasteful sprinklers.

△ **A WATERING CAN** *is a vital accessory.*

THE ESSENTIALS

An outdoor tap is a necessity for any serious gardener. It should be lagged to protect it from freezing in winter and should have a device fitted to it that prevents water flowing back into the mains. In addition, a hosepipe approximately one and a half times the length of the garden will enable you to reach every corner, allowing for detours round beds. If there are a lot of intensively cultivated beds, containers and a greenhouse, it will save time to install a simple watering system consisting of perforated pipes through which water can seep slowly, or of individual nozzles set alongside plants. This can be linked to a timing device such as a 'water computer' fixed to the tap, which automatically switches the water on and off at preset intervals – ideal for busy people or for holidays.

HOW AND WHEN TO WATER

The worst way to water is little and often. It is much better to give plants a good soaking, whether they are in containers or the open ground. Then let them drain so they are not left standing in water, and do not water again until they start to dry out. You cannot rely on

△ **SPECIAL GADGETS** *are available to divert water from downpipes into water butts to use on the garden. Several butts can be linked together.*

△ **TOMATOES ARE** *thirsty plants needing plenty of water. Insert empty pots into a growing bag so that water seeps in slowly and evenly.*

watering at regular intervals, since conditions change and plants' water needs vary. Check whether container-grown plants need watering by sticking a finger into their pots; outdoors, dig a 10cm (4in) hole with a trowel: while the surface soil may be dry, the soil further down can be moist enough. During cold weather, plants are best watered in the morning so that their foliage is dry again

before nightfall – this helps to prevent the spread of fungal disease. In hot weather, however, it is far better to water in the evening, so the plants have all night to take up the moisture before the sun comes out and evaporates it. Do not forget about watering in winter. Containers planted with winter bedding, rock plants or evergreens need watering occasionally – check them weekly.

△ GIVEN ADEQUATE MOISTURE, *healthy, well-fed plants put on a superb show in summer. A perforated pipe round the edge of this border enables shallow-rooted plants to be watered easily.*

TIPS FOR EFFICIENT WATERING

❍ Use water where it is most needed: shallow-rooted plants such as vegetables, annuals and any newly planted shrubs have top priority for watering, along with those in containers and under glass.

❍ Do not waste water on lawns: a sprinkler uses up to 250 gallons (1,000 litres) of water an hour, which is about as much as a family of four uses in the house in two days. The grass may turn brown but it grows back when autumn rains arrive. Do not feed lawns that are suffering stress as a result of water shortage; this often causes scorching.

❍ Mature trees and shrubs can fend for themselves; watering only encourages their roots to come to the surface, which in turn makes the plants less able to cope in dry conditions.

❍ Use water-retaining gel crystals in tubs and hanging baskets, and also fork them into the soil of dry flower beds, especially if they contain annual bedding plants.

❍ Make intensively cultivated deep beds for growing vegetables, salads and soft fruit, instead of growing them on a large scale, and only grow as much as you actually need – this saves both work and water.

❍ When watering new shrubs, deliver water directly to their roots by making funnels from old plastic soft drinks bottles with the base cut off, instead of splashing it over the soil surface where it evaporates quickly.

❍ Hoe regularly; weeds compete with cultivated plants for water, and hoeing creates a 'dust mulch' that helps to prevent evaporation from the moist soil deeper down.

13

DEALING WITH DROUGHT
❖❖

• Cut down on the need for watering in dry summers by deep preparation of the soil when making a new bed. Double dig, adding plenty of well-rotted organic matter to hold water.

• Make your own compost and fork as much organic matter as possible into the soil during the winter digging. Mulch beds with up to 5cm (2in) of compost or bark in autumn or early spring, while the soil is moist; do not mulch dry soil as this simply makes it harder for rain to penetrate. Use grit to mulch rock gardens.

• Install rainwater diverters to the downpipes of the house to fill up water butts or plastic barrels. This will enable you to take advantage of any showers.

• If drought is a regular occurrence in your region, consider modifying the design of your garden in order to have more paved areas instead of a thirsty lawn. You might include gravel features planted with drought-resistant shrubs and Mediterranean-style plants instead of placing the emphasis on bedding plants.

Feeding plants

In the wild, plants can live in unimproved, even poor, soil using only the recycled nutrients from dead animals and plants that decompose naturally in the earth around them. Centuries of adaptation have ensured the survival of the fittest species. But in gardens, where we grow artificially bred plants in intensively cultivated beds or in containers, plants need extra nutrients.

Bonemeal

Pellets of poultry manure

Growmore

FERTILIZERS

14

General fertilizers supply the three main nutrients – nitrogen, potassium and phosphorus – in the ideal balance. Organic products also supply minor ones, such as iron and magnesium, and trace elements. The function of each is shown in the table opposite. There are many products on sale, but you will need only a few to cover all your requirements.

△ **SOLID FERTILIZERS** *come in a variety of types and grades. Read the packet to see the exact nutrients each provides.*

▷ **PERENNIALS** *planted closely together in a flower border will benefit from being fed during the growing season if you want them to flower for as long as possible.*

△ **SPRINKLE A HANDFUL** *of general fertilizer around shrubs at the start of the growing season, following the manufacturer's instructions. Hoe well in and water if necessary.*

SOLID FERTILIZERS

Granular or powder fertilizers are designed to feed plants growing in garden beds and borders; they are mainly used when preparing the ground ready for planting but are sometimes sprinkled on and watered in for additional feeds during the growing season. Plants take up this type of feed through their roots. General fertilizers are the best for all-round use, providing a balance of all the main plant nutrients and can be used both for initial soil preparation and applied during the growing season. 'Straight', single-nutrient fertilizers are for occasional use if a particular nutrient is needed in larger amounts than the others – such as sulphate of potash to encourage flowering and fruiting of heavy-yielding crops like fruit trees and bushes.

LIQUID FEEDS

Liquid or soluble feeds have to be diluted in water. They are the best choice for plants growing in pots and other containers. Since the nutrients are already dissolved there is no risk of concentrated fertilizer touching roots and scorching them.

SLOW-RELEASE FEEDS

Slow-release feeds and fertilizer sticks or tablets are an alternative to soluble

PLANT NUTRIENTS AND THEIR BENEFITS

❖

MAJOR NUTRIENTS
Nitrogen (N): used by plants in growing healthy leaves and stems.
Potassium, potash (K): for the production of healthy flowers and fruit.
Phosphorus, phosphate (P): healthy roots.

MINOR NUTRIENTS
Iron and magnesium are ingredients of chlorophyll. Calcium builds cell walls.
Iron deficiency causes yellowing

(chlorosis) of leaves; seen when acid-lovers such as rhododendrons are not grown in acid soil.
Magnesium deficiency causes yellow leaves with green veins (seen in tomato plants and roses).
Calcium deficiency causes blossom end rot in tomatoes and bitter pit in apples; often linked to an irregular water supply.
Trace elements A huge range of other minerals are needed in minute quantities.

▽ **FOLIAR FEEDS** *are usually sprayed on to plant leaves; use them to give your plants a boost.*

feeds for containers; one application is usually enough to keep plants fed for a whole growing season.

FOLIAR FEEDS
Foliar feeds are liquid fertilizers sprayed on to leaves at low concentrations; they are a useful way to get nutrients into plants whose roots are damaged or which are in need of a tonic. Some root feeds can also be used for foliar feeding when further diluted, but check instructions.

SPECIAL-PURPOSE FEEDS
Special blends of liquid or solid feeds are sold to suit the needs of particular plants, for instance rose feeds, lawn feeds and tomato feeds. These are sometimes combined with chemical treatments – such as weedkiller in lawn feed – in which case they must be used for their intended purpose. Some have a wider use, such as high-potash liquid tomato feed, which can be used for all flowering plants as well as tomatoes. Use it for plants such as fuchsias, grown in pots and containers.

FERTILIZER DO'S AND DONT'S
15

✔ Always follow manufacturer's instructions precisely.
✘ Never exceed the recommended rate of use: excess fertilizer can scorch plant roots. If a product is over-applied by mistake, drench the soil or compost with plenty of water to wash out the excess.
✔ Apply at the start of the growing season, when the weather is good and new growth has started. Top up nutrients regularly during the growing season but tail off towards the end of it, as feeding then stimulates soft growth that may be damaged by frost.
✘ Don't apply feeds when plants are under stress due to water shortage or attack from pest or disease, nor in dormant seasons.
✔ Use solid fertilizers on moist ground, then hoe them in. If the soil surface is dry, water well in.
✘ Don't leave fertilizer granules lodged in foliage – they will scorch. Wash them off with clean water.

Choosing a lawn

Grass is the traditional choice for a lawn. But where summer water shortages make it difficult to keep grass in good condition, alternative lawns with built-in drought tolerance may be a better solution. In tiny town gardens in permanent shade or on poor clay soil, the best option may be to lay gravel or paving instead.

△ WILDFLOWER LAWNS *are cut in spring and in autumn, once all the flowers have shed their seed.*

16

▽ GENEROUS CURVES *in a lawn will enable you to manoeuvre the lawn mower effectively round them.*

GRASS LAWNS

Think carefully about your lawn from a practical as well as a visual point of view, particularly for ease of mowing. Choose a geometric shape – circle, square, hexagon or rectangle – for a formal garden or a formal feature within a different style of garden. For a country garden or an informal style of garden, choose a lawn with broad curves and possibly inset island beds. Choose meandering grass paths running through naturalistic borders in a cottage or wild-style garden. A hard path or paved edging to a lawn makes mowing easy as the mower glides over the edge of the grass; it will also prevent overhanging plants in adjacent borders from smothering the grass and causing bare or yellow patches.

WILDFLOWER LAWNS

Ideal for wildlife gardens and for more unkempt areas away from the house, a wildflower lawn is created by sowing a mixture of grass and wildflower seed, or by planting pot-grown plants into established turf and allowing them to spread naturally. Scattering packets of seed over turf does not work. Wildflower lawns are not, however, flowering versions of normal lawns – they look more like old-fashioned hay meadows. Left long, they are cut once or twice a year, in early spring and in autumn, so that the flowers can complete their life cycle and shed seed. You can achieve a wildflower effect in a domestic lawn by allowing 'weeds' such as daisies and speedwell to remain, and by refraining from using weedkillers or fertilizers. This keeps the grass growth weak but encourages wildflower species.

CLOVER LAWNS

In response to more regular hot, dry summers, clover lawns are becoming increasingly popular. Specially compact strains of white clover are sown alone or mixed with grass. The resulting 'lawn' stays green during periods of drought and makes its own nitrogen using the nitrogen-fixing nodules on the clover roots, which feed the grass growing with it. In summer, clover lawns attract bees, so take care if walking barefoot.

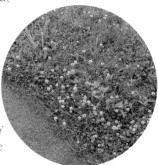

△ CLOVER LAWNS *are drought-tolerant and need little mowing as they are naturally compact.*

△ **CHAMOMILE AND THYME** *lawns make an aromatic 'carpet' but will not withstand wear.*

TURF OR SEED?

Turf is most people's first choice as it gives an instant lawn, but it is expensive and needs to be laid with care. Always choose specially cultivated turf grown from seed. Meadow turf is a cheaper option but is often full of weeds and inferior grasses. Turf can be laid on well-prepared, firmed and levelled sites from autumn through winter until late spring, as long as the soil is neither muddy nor frozen.

Seed is cheaper and usually gives better results than turf in the long run, but it takes several months to turn from a seedbed into usable lawn. The periods when grass seed can be successfully sown are limited, as it germinates best in early autumn and late spring. Various seed mixtures are available: choose hard-wearing grass for use in a family back garden, fine grass for a more ornamental lawn, and shade- or drought-tolerant mixtures for 'problem' areas.

CARING FOR NON-GRASS LAWNS

✔ Raise from plants, not seed.

✘ Do not mow: clip with shears when needed or use a hover mower to 'top' the plants lightly.

✘ Never use lawn weedkillers as they kill clovers and herbs. Hand-weed if required, though dense planting minimizes the need.

✔ Plant through a weed-barrier fabric topped with gravel to prevent weeds.

✘ Do not walk on these lawns much: they are not hard-wearing.

17

HERB LAWNS

Chamomile and thyme are the most popular choices. For chamomile lawns, choose the non-flowering variety 'Treneague', while any variety of creeping thyme, in gold, silver or green, will provide good ground cover. Both need a very well-drained, sunny site to thrive but neither will tolerate much wear. Inset 'stepping stones' of paving slabs if you need to cross the area often. Or you could make a chequerboard pattern of adjacent paving slabs and herb-planted squares for an unusual effect. When preparing the soil for a herb lawn, incorporate plenty of grit or gravel and, unless the soil is naturally fast-draining, raise the area with a 5cm (2in) layer of gravel and plant through it.

ALPINE LAWNS

A range of low, carpeting and mound-shaped rock plants are grown with clumps of dwarf bulbs to form a very decorative 'lawn'. The effect is of a Persian carpet, with colours changing throughout the seasons. But this is not a lawn for walking on – use paved or gravel paths or 'stepping stones' through it. Prepare the ground as for a herb lawn.

HEATHER CARPET

Use prostrate varieties and clumps of compact, bushy species of heather to create an undulating effect. Though it withstands some light wear, a heather carpet is safest with paths or paving running through it. It needs a sunny, well-drained soil, rich in organic matter.

Starting a new lawn

Whether you are replacing a neglected old lawn that is beyond restoration, or starting a new lawn on a bare plot, good initial site preparation is vital to its success. Thorough preparation prevents problems later on and makes the lawn easy to look after. Once grass covers the ground, it is more difficult to deal with problems like perennial weeds, poor soil or uneven ground.

CLEARING THE SITE

It is best to begin site clearance several months before you lay the lawn, to allow time for treating perennial weeds. This also enables you to tackle the heavy work in easy stages. Start by removing any builders' rubble and similar debris. Then kill the existing grass or perennial weeds by watering the area with a translocated weedkiller that acts on roots and foliage yet leaves the soil safe to sow or plant once the weeds are dead; allow six to eight weeks for this to work. Once the weeds are dead, dig or rotovate deeply, removing the roots of any perennial weeds. Leave the soil alone for a few weeks and if any weeds regrow, re-treat them as before. If annual weeds appear, simply hoe to prevent them setting seed.

IMPROVING THE GROUND

To condition the soil, spread organic matter or gritty sand (for clay soil) over the area and dig it in. Take the opportunity to level minor depressions as you work: if the site is seriously uneven, strip off the topsoil, level the

▷ **SOME GARDEN DESIGNS** *alternate areas of lawn with hard surfaces like gravel or paving, so part of the garden is usable after wet weather.*

18

subsoil, then replace the topsoil without mixing the two.

A week before sowing or turfing, sprinkle on a general fertilizer, such as blood, fish and bone or a special pre-lawn fertilizer, and rake well in. As you rake, continue levelling the soil and remove stones and debris. Then tread the area well to consolidate the soil and rake again, leaving the surface level, evenly firm with no soft spots that will sink later, and with a crumb-like surface. It may need raking several times to achieve this finish.

SOWING SEED

Timing is crucial: sow in late-spring or in early autumn. Autumn sowing is best if your summers are hot and dry, as the new grass has longer to get established before drought occurs. Choose an appropriate seed for the site and the way you intend to use the lawn: fine lawn mixtures need a high standard of regular maintenance while modern rye grasses are hard-wearing and reliable for family use. Special seed mixtures are available for shade and other difficult situations, while some have wildflower seeds added to create a wildflower lawn. Scatter the seed evenly at 25g (1oz) per square metre (practise first on a sheet of paper on the garage floor); marking the area into metre squares with canes or string makes for greater accuracy. Rake the seed into the soil surface, then water if rain does not fall within 24 hours.

LAYING TURF

This can be done any time during the winter from mid-autumn until late-spring, except when the soil is very wet and muddy or during cold, frosty weather. Cultivated turf is expensive but

LAYING TURF

❖

1 *After digging the ground deeply, sprinkle the fertilizer dressing evenly over the soil and rake well in, levelling the ground and removing stones and roots as you go.*

2 *Firm the whole area over, using your feet and allowing the weight to sink through your heels. A roller will only flatten down the peaks and leave the hollows loose.*

3 *To avoid footmarks pitting the surface of the prepared soil, work from a long plank. Start at one edge and work forwards across the area. Unroll the turves and lay them out in a row, with their edges butting tightly together.*

4 *Firm down the first row with the back of a rake. Move the plank on a little and lay the second row of turf like bricks in a wall, so the joints between adjacent turves do not run continuously. Water regularly until established.*

19

will be weed-free and of superb quality; meadow turf can be patchy and might contain weeds. The box above shows the main steps involved in laying turf.

AFTERCARE

Water thoroughly if the weather is dry, and keep off new lawns either until the turf has rooted into the soil (test by trying to lift a corner after about six weeks) or until a seed-raised lawn has had its first couple of cuts. Mow new turf as soon as it needs it. Give a seed

lawn its first cut when its longest tufts are 5cm (2in) long using hand shears, as mowers can pull new grass out. Make the next two cuts with a lightweight (that is, hover) mower with the blades set fairly high.

Do not worry about weeds in a new lawn, especially a seed-raised one; upright weeds will soon die out once regular mowing starts. Rosette weeds can be tackled later, using spot weedkiller. Avoid using weedkiller or fertilizer on new lawns for the first six months.

Routine lawn care

Grass is not difficult to keep in good condition and establishing a routine of basic care, mainly involving regular mowing and feeding, will help you to maintain a green, dense and problem-free lawn. A well cared-for lawn will also withstand drought and wear better than a lawn that is left to struggle.

MOWING

Mow once a week or more in summer, and once a month in winter. Not only does this keep a lawn tidy, it also helps to thicken the grass up and deters weeds; regular topping should control all upright weeds without the use of weedkillers. For normal lawns, 2–2.5cm (¾–1in) is the shortest you need mow them, cutting a little shorter on fine-quality lawns. Alter the height of cut by adjusting the mower blades to leave grass 1.2cm (½in) longer in winter and during dry spells in summer, reducing the height again when growing conditions improve.

Always trim round lawn edges after mowing to keep the grass looking neat, using either edging shears, an electric lawn edger or a suitable rotating line trimmer. Properly made lawn edges allow easier trimming and prevent grass 'creeping' into the surrounding borders. To maintain clean edges, go round the lawn with a spade or half-moon edger every spring, pulling away the soil to leave a firm vertical edge to the turf, 5–7.5cm (2–3in) deep.

FEEDING

Feeding grass keeps it green and thick. Thinning and patchy grass encourages the growth of weeds as seed can germinate more easily in bare soil; seedlings get smothered in dense grass, which acts like a living mulch. Use a high-nitrogen lawn feed in late spring, substituting a combined feed-and-weed or moss treatment product (if either are a problem bear in mind that small patches of weed or moss can be individually spot-treated). The late spring feed is the most important one. If lawns receive heavy wear, for instance small family lawns or those used for games or sports in additional to normal use, it is advisable to repeat regular lawn feeds

△ HOLD LONG-HANDLED SHEARS *vertically, pressing the blade close to the lawn to get a clean cut. Keep the lower blade horizontal, holding its handle still; use the upper blade to cut.*

◁ TO GIVE A LAWN *the traditional striped effect, use a cylinder mower and turn it at the end of each strip, working back in the opposite direction.*

△ IF THE SOIL IS DRY, *apply liquid lawn feed, using a hand-held dilutor that fits on to the end of a hosepipe. Liquid feed also gives lawns a boost.*

every six weeks until midsummer. In autumn, treat lawns to a programme of care designed to help them through winter and prepare them for next year. Start by raking well, either by hand or

---

ROTARY TRIMMERS
❖

These are handy machines for trimming long grass where a lawn butts up against a fence or wall, or where a mower will not reach. Do not use round trees or hedges as the spinning line can cut into the bark and damage it. Most trimmers are electric but petrol versions are available. Follow the usual safety precautions.

---

with a mechanical raker, to remove moss and thatch-like debris that accumulates round the base of grass stems. The material gathered can be composted. Regular treading down of a lawn compacts it, which closes air spaces in the soil, causing poor drainage and an unhealthy lawn, so spike in autumn to relieve any compaction (*see left*). Finish by applying a specially formulated autumn lawn fertilizer containing very little nitrogen, encouraging good root action rather than lush, leafy growth. On heavy clay soils, a light top-dressing of fine grit helps to leave a firm surface that does not get muddy in wet weather and assists surface drainage. Other lawns can be improved by top-dressing with sifted compost or rich soil. Apply a bucketful per square metre, and work it in with the back of a rake or a besom broom, so as not to smother the grass.

△ HOLLOW-TINE SPIKERS
remove entire cores of soil each time they are pressed down into the soil. Sweep up the deposited soil, then brush grit into the holes left in the lawn, to improve both aeration and drainage.

DO'S AND DON'TS FOR THE BEST RESULTS

✔ Use a spreader to ensure even application of granular products, which are not easy to apply by hand. Measure out liquid products carefully and dilute at the correct rate. Mark the lawn out into metre squares using string, to ensure accurate application.

✔ Water in granular feed and lawn treatments if it does not rain within 48 hours after applying them. Or use a liquid formulation that does not need watering in.

✘ Do not use lawn weedkillers just before it rains. The product, taken in through weed leaves, needs 12 hours or more in which to work – it is de-activated in the soil.

✔ Use an autumn formulation lawn fertilizer in spring and summer instead of the usual feed if you want to thicken up the grass without encouraging lush green growth that will need more mowing.

✔ Buy a separate watering can to use only for applying liquid lawn weedkillers; however well you wash out a can, the tiny traces that remain are enough to harm sensitive plants.

✘ Do not use lawn feeds, even liquid products, on a lawn that has turned brown due to drought. They will not help and may make things worse by scorching the grass. Wait until after prolonged rain when the grass has started to grow again naturally, then rake out the worst of the dead grass and apply half-strength lawn feed.

21

Dealing with lawn problems

A perfect lawn sets off the whole garden; conversely, one that is obviously suffering can make even the best-kept garden look somewhat neglected. If you treat lawn problems correctly and as soon as they are spotted, most of them will be quickly and easily cured.

△ **SLICES OF LOG**
make good natural 'stepping stones' across a lawn.

22

ERADICATING WEEDS

Weeds are generally a problem where grass is thin or has bare patches; regular feeding thickens grass so weeds cannot get a foothold. Upright weeds are rarely a problem in lawns as frequent mowing weakens and kills them. The commonest lawn weeds are low-growing rosettes and mat-forming kinds like daisies, dandelion, creeping buttercup, clover, speedwell and trefoil that pass safely under the blades of a mower. Tackle broad-leaved weeds individually, using spot lawn weedkiller. If a large area needs treating, use liquid weedkiller or granular feed-and-weed treatments. Clover, speedwell and trefoil are harder to kill; use a liquid product specially for small-leaved lawn weeds, or dig them out singly with a trowel or daisy grubber. Mat-forming weeds like trefoil come out easily if you find the centre of the plant and twist until the roots come out.

▽ **VISUALLY,** *a lawn is the outdoor equivalent of carpet in the living room. It too needs regular care to keep it hardwearing and looking its best.*

▷ GRASS PATHS *are susceptible to excess wear. Firm the surface by sprinkling gritty sand to stop it going muddy in wet weather.*

DEALING WITH MOSS

Moss tends to be a problem in shade, damp areas, badly compacted soil, or where the grass is scalped by a mower cutting too close over bumps in the lawn. Firstly, you need to improve the lawn's drainage and relieve any compaction in order to deter the invasion of moss. Moss can, however, occur in any lawn after a wet winter. Treat it using a liquid mosskiller or combined granular feed-and-mosskiller product for lawns in mid-spring. Moss turns black when dead and should then be raked out. Live moss is harder to remove, and small fragments will remain and regrow.

ALGAE AND LIVERWORT

These are mostly a problem on heavy clay soils during wet weather, when the lawn can become dangerously slippery. Rake or scrape off the worst, then hollow-tine spike the lawn or slash the area and brush gritty sand into the holes to improve surface drainage. Some brands of liquid lawn mosskillers also kill algae and liverwort: check the information on the packet.

FAIRY RINGS

True fairy rings are persistent circles of small toadstools that are present all year, shrivelling up in summer but rehydrating after rain. The circles slowly get bigger, leaving weak yellow grass inside and a ring of lush, bright green grass just outside that of the fungi. There is no easy cure; you will need to dig out soil from the ring to a depth of 45cm (18in), treat

with a phenol-based soil sterilant if available, fill the hole with new topsoil and re-turf. Occasional toadstools in autumn are nothing to worry about and they vanish at the first frost.

DAMAGE CAUSED BY WEAR

Regular use in one direction will wear a bare 'path' across a lawn and you would do best to lay a hard path or stepping stones over your route to the shed, garage or compost heap. If you need to push heavy barrows over the lawn in wet weather, avoid making ruts by unrolling a temporary 'path' of heavy-grade plastic netting where and when it is needed.

REPAIRING BROKEN EDGES

Replace collapsed or torn lawn edges by cutting out a square of turf that includes the broken area. Turn it round and fit it back into the gap, so the 'hole' is now inside the lawn, leaving a firm outer edge to the lawn. Fill hole with seed compost or fine garden soil, sprinkle grass seed over, rake it into the surface and water.

DEALING WITH DROUGHT

During prolonged drought grass turns first yellow, then brown. It is rarely actually dead and will soon recover once autumn rains start. Do not feed a lawn during drought to try and turn it green

– it simply makes things worse by scorching it. Once the rain comes, spike the lawn thoroughly to assist water penetration (rain is slow to sink into bone-dry lawns and often just lays on the top and evaporates). Do not feed until after the grass has greened up naturally.

YELLOW PATCHES

These have various causes. If you see a bitch use the lawn, dilute the urine with a bucket of water. Avoid petrol spills from the mower by refuelling it on a hard surface, not on the grass, and fill fertilizer spreaders on the path too, as spills scorch the grass.

OVERALL NEGLECT

It is usually cheaper and easier to restore a neglected lawn than to replace it. Follow a routine of regular cutting, feeding with lawn feed at six-weekly intervals from mid-spring to midsummer and treating in spring to eradicate moss or weeds, followed by the full autumn care programme outlined on page 21.

23

SEEDING WORN PATCHES

❖

Balding patches spoil the appearance of a lawn, allow weeds to colonize and make it muddier in wet weather. The solution is to reseed thin or patchy areas in spring or autumn. Rake off dead grass and loosen soil with the points of a fork. Sprinkle on grass seed and scuffle in, then water well and cover with netting.

Planting a hedge

A hedge is the traditional garden surround. A living boundary, it is more permanent than fencing but needs more space and greater upkeep. Depending on the type of hedge and the plant chosen, a hedge can provide a year-round backdrop for other plants, a dense, evergreen barrier, an informal flowering boundary or a neat dwarf edging to beds or paths.

△ **HEDGES DO NOT** *have to be straight; this curved hedge of* Berberis thunbergii *makes an architectural feature leading to the flight of steps.*

SOIL AND SITUATION

Always choose hedging plants that like the conditions in your garden. On a chalky soil and an exposed site, beech is the best choice; otherwise, *Lonicera nitida* is good for most exposed situations. Conifer hedges need a soil that is well-drained but never dries out badly, as this can cause browning of the foliage. In shade, choose box, which needs only a few hours of direct sunlight each day. Beech and hornbeam which, though not evergreen, retain their brown leaves in winter, are the favourites for a traditional garden. Evergreen hedges such as yew or box make an ideal backing for a herbaceous border and are also suitable for dividing a large garden into 'rooms'. Yew can be clipped to as little as 30cm (12in) wide and, being slow-growing, clipping need be done only once a year, in late summer. Good seaside hedges include escallonia and *Griselinia littoralis*; in mild regions, hardy fuchsias make colourful boundaries.

THE HEIGHT

Select plants that are appropriate for the height of hedge required. No hedge will stop at a certain height but some, such as thuja, make an easily maintained, low to medium hedge, while Leylands cypress needs regular, severe pruning to keep it to a reasonable height; yew, beech, hornbeam and privet are also suitable for tall hedges. Informal, flowering hedges should be chosen with regard to the natural size of the plants used as they are pruned only lightly to permit flowering, and cannot be cut hard to keep them shorter. For a low or medium hedge of around 1m (3ft), choose box, berberis, thuja or *Prunus cistena*. For an informal, low edging to beds or paths, choose naturally compact, slow-growing plants such as santolina or lavender.

BUYING PLANTS

Popular hedging plants such as beech and hornbeam can often be bought inexpensively between late autumn and spring as bare-rooted plants; they must be planted during the dormant season. First soak the roots in tepid water for eight hours to rehydrate the plants and 'heel' them into a patch of ground if they cannot be planted straight away. Suitable shrubs for hedging, including berberis, shrub roses and conifers like thuja, are normally only sold as

---

WHICH HEDGE PLANT?

❖

FORMAL EVERGREEN
yew, holly, thuja, box, privet,
Lonicera nitida
FORMAL DECIDUOUS
beech, hornbeam, Prunus cistena
'Crimson Dwarf'
INFORMAL FLOWERING
Rosa rugosa, *forsythia, spiraea,*
berberis, escallonia, hebe
PRICKLY
(LIVESTOCK- AND INTRUDER-PROOF)
hawthorn, holly, pyracantha,
berberis, species roses
DWARF
dwarf box (Buxus sempervirens
'Suffruticosa'), *lavender, rosemary,*
cotton lavender (Santolina)
MIXED WILDLIFE
hawthorn, hazel, elder, dog rose,
blackthorn

plants represent the best value as they establish faster than large plants and grow rapidly to catch up with them.

PLANTING

Plant formal hedges of beech, hornbeam, hawthorn and privet in double rows 38–45cm (15–18in) apart, with plants the same distance apart in the row but staggered, to produce a dense, solid hedge quickly.

Plant conifers and bushy shrubs in a single line 38–45cm (15–18in) apart. Before planting, dig a trench 1m (3ft) wide and fork as much well-rotted organic matter or tree planting compost as possible into the bottom. Add general fertilizer and bonemeal at the manufacturer's recommended rate and

mix thoroughly into the soil before replacing it in the trench. Plant hedging plants in the same way as for normal garden shrubs.

AFTERCARE

To avoid having a hedge that is bare at the base, cut plants back hard after planting. Prune bare-rooted plants to 15cm (6in) above ground and container-grown plants by one-third. This encourages vigorous branching from the base, which produces a dense, strong, well-shaped hedge with leaves down to the ground. Feed in spring by scattering general fertilizer or rose food along each side of the hedge, if possible, and watering it well in. Remove weeds and ivy from the base of the hedge regularly and mulch in spring, especially while the hedge is young.

container-grown plants, making a hedge quite expensive. However, they can be planted at most times of year, except when the ground is frosty, muddy or during drought, when plants are difficult to establish. Spring and autumn are ideal planting times. Small

25

◁ PLANT A PRIVET HEDGE *into well-prepared soil: once in place, a hedge can last many decades and this is the only chance you will have to improve growing conditions. Cut hard back after planting to create a hedge that will be fully clothed with foliage right down to the ground.*

Trimming hedges

From the time it is planted, a hedge needs trimming correctly to encourage it to form a good shape and to keep the plants leafy to ground level. Depending on the type of hedge, it will subsequently need regular clipping or pruning to keep it neat, shapely and within bounds. The right technique and good-quality tools make the job easy and efficient.

CREATING A NEW HEDGE

After planting and cutting hard back, clip little and often, perhaps four to six times in the second year after planting, depending on the plant's speed of growth; aim to remove the tips of the new growth to encourage plenty of side shoots to develop. As the hedge grows taller, shape it so that it is slightly wider at the base than the top – a top-heavy hedge can splay open after rain or snow and, if the base is shaded by the overhanging top, the bottom of the main stems soon become bare. Use a line held up by poles as a cutting guide to ensure the height of the hedge is level.

ESTABLISHED FORMAL HEDGES

Once the hedge reaches the required height, it will need less frequent clipping. Slow-growing hedges like beech, box and yew usually need cutting only twice, in early summer and late summer. Fast-growing hedges like *Lonicera nitida* and privet require regular clipping between late spring and late summer, every time the hedge starts to look shaggy, usually about every six weeks. Start clipping from the base of the hedge and work your way up, as this makes it easier to shape the sides correctly. Prune large-leaved hedges such as laurel with secateurs rather than clipping them with shears or a hedge trimmer, so that leaves are not cut in half.

INFORMAL HEDGES

After planting, informal flowering hedges should be hard pruned to a third of their

△ **LAUREL IS** *a popular hedging plant but has large leaves which, when cut in half by hedge trimmers, turn brown and unsightly. Instead use secateurs and remove straggly shoots by hand.*

height, to encourage them to thicken up at the base. Thereafter they are not clipped to give straight edges like a formal hedge, but instead are pruned to retain the natural shape of the plant. As a general rule, prune hedges that flower before early summer, such as forsythia or ribes, immediately after flowering, and later-flowering hedges, such as roses, in mid-spring. Country-style hedges are also usually pruned to keep them tidy; for a more natural look, a hedge of hawthorn could be formally clipped, but leaving occasional plants to grow up through the hedge to develop into trees.

26

HEDGE-TRIMMING TOOLS

❖

SHEARS: hand shears are good for small formal hedges but tiring to use over large areas; use sheep shears for dwarf flowering hedges.

SECATEURS: use for informal flowering hedges and large-leaved plants such as laurel.

POWER HEDGE-TRIMMERS: these are the most practical option for large areas of hedging. Cordless types need recharging often but are ideal for small areas, while electric models with cables are the most popular.

PETROL-DRIVEN HEDGE-TRIMMERS: these are expensive and heavy to use but useful for large hedges a long way from a power point. Consider hiring someone to cut your hedges as an alternative to buying expensive specialist equipment.

CLIPPING FOR TOPIARY

Box and yew are the favourite subjects for topiary. Since both are slow-growing, once their shape is established they can usually be maintained with two clips a year, in early and late summer; clip more often if this is necessary to maintain a clear outline. When creating new topiary, use an internal framework of poles or wire netting to support large or complicated shapes; small- to medium-sized simple shapes with a wide base and a domed outline can remain unsupported. While training a new shape, clip 4–6 times a year using hand shears, removing the tips of new shoots to encourage side shoots to thicken it out. If you are training into a complicated shape, use secateurs to prune fiddly features.

△ **YEW TOPIARY** *is trained into formal geometric cubes, with mophead hollies emerging from them.*

DWARF HEDGES

Clip formal dwarf box in early and late summer using sheep shears to keep it tidy. Flowering dwarf hedges, such as lavender and santolina, should be lightly clipped with sheep shears immediately after flowering to remove dead flowerheads and re-shape the plants, but without cutting back into old wood, which can kill them. Rosemary may be either pruned or clipped after flowering, depending on the growth habit of the variety used: dense, bushy forms are best clipped with shears, while upright or open types should be pruned using secateurs to prevent spoiling the natural shape of the shrub or leaving leaves cut in half, which will then turn brown.

◁ **PETROL-DRIVEN** *powered hedge clippers are convenient for a large garden too far from a power point to use electric models, but they are heavy to use and expensive to buy. You could hire the equipment or let a contractor cut hedges for you. Wear gloves and goggles to use safely.*

SAFETY TIPS

LADDERS: when clipping tall hedges, place two pairs of stepladders securely on level ground with a plank between them and make sure it is stable before starting work; ask someone to hold ladders stable. Purpose-made pruning platforms are also available.

ELECTRIC CABLE: make sure electric cable is secured over your shoulder and well out of the way of blades when using powered hedge-trimmers; plug into a RCD so the current switches off instantly in case of accidents.

Planting and caring for trees

Trees add impact and height to a garden, cast desirable shade or provide a feature on a boundary or in the middle of a lawn. Choose a tree with care to ensure that it does not outgrow its space, deprive nearby plants of nutrients or cause any structural damage. Fortunately, there are plenty of attractive, small to medium-sized ornamental trees that are easy to maintain.

CHOOSING A TREE

Forest and parkland trees are unsuitable for most gardens, as they grow far too big, create dense shade beneath which nothing grows, and remove large volumes of water daily from the soil when they are in leaf. It is better to choose a decorative garden tree with a compact habit and small root system. Check nursery labels or reference books to find a tree's ultimate height and spread, to see whether it is a suitable size for your garden. Avoid large willow species near drains as their roots seek water and can cause obstructions.

When buying, select a tree with a symmetrical shape, with five or more strong branches evenly spaced round the trunk. A tree with a lopsided head or a bent trunk can be improved once it is planted but it takes several years to rectify serious defects; better to have a tree that earns its keep in the garden from the start. (In wild or cottage-style gardens, craggy, asymmetrically shaped trees add character, so in this case you might choose a misshapen tree deliberately and prune it to exaggerate the effect.) Check that the foliage is healthy and the trunk undamaged, with sound bark from top to bottom.

PLANTING A TREE

Dig a hole at least twice the size of the tree's rootball, fork plenty of organic matter into the bottom and mix in some general fertilizer or, in autumn or winter, bonemeal. If the soil is prone to waterlogging, dig over the whole area to improve a wide root-run, adding grit or bark chippings for aeration.

Water the tree well before removing it from its pot. If it is pot-bound, with roots wound tightly round the inside of the pot, gently tease a few large roots out from the mass.

Stand the tree in the hole, and check that the top of the rootball is level with the surrounding soil. Hammer in a short tree stake alongside the rootball. Fill round the roots with a mix of good topsoil and organic matter.

Firm gently, water well and, when any sinkage has taken place, use tree ties

---

28

BEST TREES FOR SMALL GARDENS

❖

Good trees for small plots include birch, *Crataegus* 'Paul's Scarlet', snowy mespilus (*Amelanchier lamarckii*), crab apples (*Malus*), mulberry (*Morus nigra*) and Cheal's weeping cherry (*Prunus* 'Kidu-shidare-zakura'). For something more unusual try *Gleditsia triacanthos* 'Sunburst', with golden, cut-leaf foliage and 'Ruby Lace', whose red foliage turns bronze-green, or *Caragana arborescens* with yellow pea flowers which reaches 3.5m (12ft) and is ideal for windy or coastal sites.

◁ **THE GOLDEN ROBINIA** (R. pseudoacacia *'Frisia') makes an outstanding medium-sized tree for a sunny situation. It thrives in dry soil so is ideal for areas prone to summer drought.*

them, especially the area overhung by the edge of the canopy of branches since this is where the 'feeding' roots are. Mulch round trees with a 2.5–5cm (1–2in) layer of any well-rotted organic material or bark chippings. Grass competes with young trees for water and nutrients so leave established trees grown in grass with a ring of soil round the trunk at least 90cm (3ft) across. Keep new trees well watered in summer but leave established ones to take care of themselves. A late-summer feed high in potash and phosphates (such as liquid tomato feed) will help to ripen the current year's growth and encourage spring-flowering trees to produce buds. Prune trees only if it is necessary to remove damaged, diseased or overcrowded growth.

TREES IN SMALL SPACES

❖

Where space is short, consider cutting back suitable trees to rejuvenate them when they get too big. Done every 2–3 years, this even makes them grow as shrubs. *Acer negundo* 'Flamingo', with pretty pink, cream and green variegated leaves, can be cut back almost to ground level in spring when it gets too big. The same can be done with eucalyptus and the Judas tree (*Cercis siliquastrum*) to keep them bushy instead of letting them turn into a tree. Or use large shrubs such as the strawberry tree (*Arbutus unedo*), *Garrya elliptica* or *Clerodendrum trichotomum* 'Fargesii' and remove their lower branches to turn them into small standard trees.

29

to hold the trunk against the stake. Check that the buffer is between trunk and stake to prevent the bark chafing. Finally, mulch with a 2.5–5cm (1–2in) layer of bark chippings or garden compost to retain moisture.

TREE CARE

In mid-spring, at the start of the growing season, when the soil is moist, feed and mulch both newly planted and established trees. Sprinkle general fertilizer or rose food evenly around

△ **USE A PRUNING SAW** *to reshape a lopsided or overgrown tree: remove an entire branch at its junction with the trunk or a larger branch.*

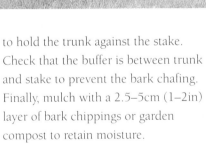

△ **LEAVE A GRASS-FREE** *circle around trees in lawns to prevent competition for water and nutrients. Mulch in spring to retain moisture.*

Planting and moving shrubs

Shrubs flesh out the framework of the garden. Depending on type, they can fill large areas quickly, or supply seasonal flowers for mixed borders – particularly useful in early summer – as well as fruit, berries or foliage tints in late summer. Evergreen shrubs are invaluable for providing all-year-round effects.

30

PLANTING A CONTAINER-GROWN SHRUB
❖

- Prepare the planting site by digging in plenty of well-rotted organic matter such as garden compost or manure if making a new bed; in previously well-cultivated soil, dig a hole at least twice the size of the pot the plant is growing in and fork well-rotted compost into the bottom of it.

- Water the shrub well before knocking it out of its pot, and if the rootball appears to be a solid mass of roots, gently tease out a few large roots, otherwise they will not be able to break loose after planting and the shrub will remain in virtually suspended animation.

- Turn the shrub so that its best side faces the front and place in the hole, with the top of the rootball roughly flush with the soil surface.

- Fill in round the roots with a mixture of good topsoil and well-rotted organic matter, firm gently and water well to settle the soil round the roots. Keep watered in dry spells.

CHOOSING HEALTHY SHRUBS

Look for symmetrically shaped plants with plenty of evenly spaced branches and healthy green leaves; avoid leggy or lopsided specimens as it takes time and heavy pruning to rectify defects. If the surface of the container is covered with moss, liverwort or weeds, this may indicate that the plant has been on sale for some time. If the

◁ JAPANESE MAPLES *(Acer palmatum) and cultivars such as 'Garnet' make spectacular small specimen trees. They thrive in well-drained but moisture-retentive soil and light shade.*

leaves also look pale or stunted, or dead twigs or leaves are present, then suspect generally poor care and wait until you can find a better specimen.

WHEN TO PLANT

Autumn is generally the best time to plant, since this allows new shrubs to get established while the soil is naturally warm and moist; container-grown shrubs can, however, be planted at any time of year except when the soil is very muddy, frosty or suffering from drought. Late spring and early autumn are the best times for planting evergreens; if they experience water shortage after planting they lose their leaves and take a long time to recover; conifers often go brown round the base and may never replace the damage with new foliage.

MOVING SHRUBS

Sometimes it becomes necessary to move a shrub that has been planted in the garden for a long time, perhaps due to overcrowding. Certain shrubs, such as magnolia, resent disturbance and should never be moved but most can be moved with care. The ideal time to move deciduous shrubs is in early spring, just before the start of the growing season, though they can be moved at any time between leaf fall in autumn and bud burst in spring. Small, shallow-rooted or recently planted shrubs can simply be dug up with a large ball of roots and moved to a new, well-prepared site, in one go. Keep them well watered after the move.

Large or well-established shrubs

In the case of large or long-established plants, it is best to start preparing for a move a year or more in advance. The previous autumn or spring, dig a narrow trench 60cm (2ft) deep round the plant, about as far from the trunk as the outermost branches extend. Cut through any large roots you find, and cut under the plant to sever any thick tap roots at that depth. Then fill the trench with a mixture of good topsoil and planting compost or well-rotted organic matter to encourage fibrous roots to form. A year or more later, the shrub will have grown the sort of root system that allows it to be moved safely. Lift with as much fibrous root as possible, have the new site well prepared and sit the shrub in place straight away. Keep well watered.

Evergreen shrubs and conifers

Early autumn is the best time of year to move evergreens and conifers; water thoroughly a few days before moving them. Dig them up with plenty of roots and transfer immediately to the new, well-prepared planting hole. Use temporary stakes to prevent wind-rock

△ **EVEN LARGE RHODODENDRONS** *move surprisingly well since they have a shallow root system. If you have time, prepare the plant a year in advance to encourage it to grow lots of new, fibrous roots into a compost-rich trench.*

until well established and protect with a surrounding windbreak for their first winter. In an exposed situation, spray plants with anti-transpirant spray to reduce moisture loss through their leaves (often sold in autumn to prevent Christmas trees shedding their needles).

MOVING A SMALL SHRUB

❖

1 *Dig the shrub up carefully with a large rootball and lift it on to a polythene sheet (use this for surplus soil too, to protect a lawn).*

2 *Drag the plant on the plastic sheet to its new home. Have the planting hole ready-prepared and lift in place, then replace the soil.*

Using climbers

Growing climbing plants is a wonderful way to cover bare walls and fences or to mask unsightly outbuildings. Climbers can also be trained over arches and pergolas, or against a framework of poles or pillars to give height to the back of a border. And you can grow climbers up through unproductive old fruit trees – and through each other – to make the most of every vertical space.

▷ **CLEMATIS, ROSES**
*and honeysuckle
grown together in the
same space create a
varied tapestry effect.*

32

▽ **OBELISKS** *make
an attractive support
for decorative
climbers grown in
a border.*

CLIMBERS TO CLOTHE VERTICAL FEATURES

Climbing roses, honeysuckle or clematis are the traditional choice for arches, arbours and pergolas and scent is an important factor to take into account. But consider unusual alternatives too, such as *Trachelospermum asiaticum*, a slightly tender, evergreen climber with fragrant white flowers in summer, and summer jasmine (*Jasminum officinale*), a cottage-style climber with heavily scented white flowers. The purple grape, *Vitis vinifera* 'Purpurea', and the pink-, cream- and green-variegated *Ampelopsis*

glandulosa var. *brevipedunculata* 'Elegans' add foliage contrast. Grow two or three climbers together for a generous effect – most kinds team well with climbing roses.

For pillars, choose smaller-growing climbing or rambler roses, and wind the stems round so they 'concertina' all round the pillar instead of growing straight up. This allows more of the stem to grow horizontally, and it is on this growth that most flowers are produced, so the pillar will bloom all the way up, instead of only at the top.

Choose large, vigorous climbers to ramble up through trees and make an impact quickly. Suitable choices for large trees include species clematis, strong rambler or climbing roses such as 'Rambling Rector', the vine, *Vitis coignetiae* and *Celastrus scandens* (bittersweet). Clematis are ideal for colonizing old fruit trees, and not-too-vigorous kinds look effective twining their way among the 'arms' of espaliers or interwoven through fruit tunnels.

GROWING AGAINST WALLS

Where climbers would be too vigorous or tend to get out of control, wall shrubs often make a good substitute. Shrubs such as glossy, small-leaved pyracantha or ornamental quince (*Chaenomeles*) can be trained as a narrow fan, espalier or bush shape more or less flat against a wall, where they make a pleasing outline. It is also a good idea to grow lax shrubs, such as *Abeliophyllum distichum* (which has almond-scented flowers in spring) and winter jasmine (*Jasminum nudiflorum*), against a wall, as they flop untidily otherwise. Where there is plenty of room, large wall shrubs like the evergreen *Magnolia grandiflora* and the pineapple broom (*Cytisus battandieri*) make a dramatic feature.

CLIMBERS IN CONTAINERS

❖

Many climbers need more root-room than containers permit but clematis make excellent subjects for tubs and large (45cm/18in) pots; check the label and choose those, such as *C. florida* 'Sieboldii', that do not grow too big. Plant in loam-based compost and push trellis or an obelisk into the pot for the plant to grow up. Keep well fed with liquid tomato feed during the growing season and place where their roots will be in cool shade, perhaps surrounded by other planted containers or with pebbles on the top of the compost.

CREATING A SCREEN

❖

The fastest way to create a living screen is not to plant a hedge, but to grow climbers up a fence or trellis support. In this way you can achieve the desired height instantly, with a reasonable degree of plant cover within the first growing season, yet the screen never grows too tall and any trimming can be done quite conveniently. Choose a mixture of climbers such as winter jasmine and ivy for a country-garden look or all of the same kind for a more hedge-like effect, for example *Clematis armandii*. Vigorous, fast-growing climbers such as Virginia creeper or wisteria are quite suitable for large screens but lose their leaves in winter. Include some evergreen climbers, such as ivies or euonymus, for all-year-round cover. A slightly slower alternative is to grow wall shrubs in the same way and trim them closely for a dense, more formal appearance: pyracantha is stunning grown in this way.

Shady walls

A few climbing roses are happy on a shady wall: choose red 'Danse du Feu', maroon 'Souvenir du Dr Jamain' or yellow 'Mermaid'. Climbing hydrangea (*H. petiolaris*) and its relative *Schizophragma* will thrive on a cool wall, as do wall-trained *Garrya elliptica* and winter jasmine. Team the latter with large-leaved, variegated ivies for good effect. In deeper shade, use varieties of euonymus, which climbs modestly when grown against a wall.

◁ **WHEN GROWING** *climbers against a wall or fence that is likely to need maintenance, fix trellis to the wall and train the climber to it.*

Sunny walls

Save this very desirable habitat for slightly tender plants in need of protection and a warm, sunny spot: these include climbers such as passion flower (*Passiflora caerulea*), campsis, Chilean potato vine (*Solanum*), parrot-bill (*Clianthus puniceus*) or *Rosa banksiae*, and wall-trained shrubs *Fremontodendron californica*, myrtle or ceanothus. Look out too for more unusual candidates such as *Billadiera longiflora*, which has large, decorative, blue berries. If a severe cold spell threatens, it is quite easy to secure frost-protection fleece to the wall and drop it down over the plants.

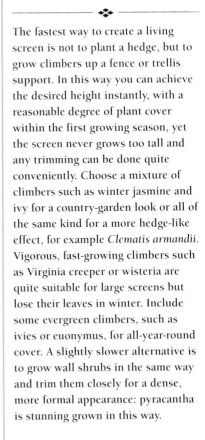

33

Growing climbers

The growing conditions where climbers are usually planted are not naturally good. At the base of walls, for example, the soil is often full of rubble while under trees, spreading tree roots create dry, impoverished conditions. And both walls and trees tend to deflect rain from the soil. Since climbers will live in the same spot for many years, it is worth taking trouble over soil preparation before planting them.

PLANTING AGAINST A WALL

When planting a climber at the foot of a wall, you need to do more than just prepare a planting hole; you must improve the entire bed to give the climber a good root-run. Remove as much rubble as possible and deeply dig in plenty of well-rotted organic matter; if the soil is really poor or full of builder's debris, replace it with good-quality topsoil. Put up supports before planting, since it is much harder to do so afterwards. Dig a deep hole and plant so that the main stem is 45cm (18in) away from the wall; insert a stake and lean it against the wall for the plant to grow along. Be prepared to water in dry spells while plants are young, as the base of a wall, especially a south-facing one, is always a dry site.

PLANTING UNDER A TREE

When planting a climber to grow up through a tree, choose a spot on the north side of the tree if possible, as the climber will grow towards the light; if it is planted on the bright side of the tree, it may refuse to climb. Prepare a very large planting hole, as you will need to allow room to work round the tree roots, and

▷ **VIRGINIA CREEPER** *looks wonderful framing the windows and doors of old stone houses, especially in its autumn colours.*

mix in plenty of organic matter with the soil. Plant at least 60cm (2ft) from the trunk of a small tree. If the tree is large, plant just under the outermost extent of its canopy of branches, at the 'drip line', where there is more light and water. Incline a stake from the base of the

---

PLANTING A CLIMBER

❖

1 *Dig a planting hole about twice the size of the plant's rootball and add well-rotted organic matter mixed with general fertilizer.*

2 *Check the depth of the hole: clematis should be planted so that the rootball is about 15cm (6in) below the soil surface.*

3 *Tease out a few of the thickest roots if the plant is slightly pot-bound. Put in place and fill with topsoil mixed with rotted organic matter.*

climber to the trunk or up into the lower branches, fix firmly in place and use this to 'lead' the plant up on to its support.

TRAINING CLIMBERS

New plants can be shy to start climbing. To encourage self-clinging species,

4 *Untie the plant stems from the cane and spread them out in a wide fan, with the bottom stems almost horizontal; tie in place.*

FORMS OF SUPPORT

❖

Some climbers, like ivy and Virginia creeper, support themselves using aerial roots that cling to bare walls; avoid growing these on crumbly surfaces as the aerial roots can make them worse. Other plants, such as honeysuckle and clematis, will twine or cling to supports with their leaf-stems without needing to be tied; trellis or rigid netting fixed to the wall or fence is ideal for these. Climbers such as roses, as well as fan-trained trees and wall shrubs with stiff stems, need tying in place: horizontal wires stretched at 30cm (12in) intervals up the wall, or wall nails outlining the shape of the plant's framework, are the best methods of support.

dampen the wall with water, especially on hot days. Twiners and clingers often need a little persuasion too; after planting, tie the stems up to their support with soft string and from then on they should manage without help. When growing up brick pillars or the uprights of a pergola, fix netting in place to give them something to grip on to.

Stiff-stemmed climbers like roses need to be tied in regularly during the growing season to stop them drooping down the wall and becoming untidy. Tie in their stems every 45cm (18in) or so, and check that the ties are not cutting into the stems as they thicken. Train roses and wall shrubs so their main stems are evenly spaced over the area of wall to be covered and use this as the framework to which they are pruned every year.

TRAINING TIPS

❍ Do not allow wisteria to grow round drainpipes or gutters: its woody stems expand as they grow and can force pipes off the wall.

❍ Wooden fences need occasional maintenance in the form of timber treatment and garden walls need repainting, so it is a good idea to grow climbers on trellis; this can be detached and laid flat on the ground, complete with climber, for access to the fence or wall.

❍ Space trellis or support wires 10cm (4in) from a wall to allow air circulation between the plant and the wall. This stops the plant from overheating and prevents problems associated with damp. Use vine eyes to carry the wires or fix cotton reels between wall and trellis to maintain the necessary distance.

❍ Keep climbing roses and honeysuckle well watered in dry spells to prevent mildew on their foliage; this can be a symptom of dryness at the roots.

❍ If climbers become bare at the base, use their bare stems as a support for fast-growing decorative annual climbers such as asarina or canary creeper (*Tropaeolum peregrinum*).

❍ Container-grown climbers sold in flower at garden centres may not bloom again for several years after planting as a result of the plant being given a larger root-run. This is not a cause for concern since it will generally start flowering again as soon as it is well established. It is not uncommon for a wisteria to take seven years before it begins flowering.

35

Planting and caring for herbaceous borders

Herbaceous plants are those that die down every autumn, spend the winter as dormant roots underground, then send up new shoots in spring. Traditionally, they were always grown in herbaceous borders – large, formal beds backed by a hedge or fence. But in small gardens, informal-shaped island beds surrounded by lawn are a popular and more practical way of growing them, or individual plants may be grown in containers.

PLANTING HERBACEOUS PERENNIALS

36

Herbaceous plants bought container-grown at the garden centre can theoretically be put in at most times of year, but the best season to plant is in spring, when the first shoots are visible but before there is much leafy growth. This way you can be certain that the pot contains a live plant (it is not always easy to tell in autumn or winter when the foliage has died down), and the plant has some time in which to get established before starting to flower. If you plant it when in flower, you can expect a fairly short flowering season. All herbaceous plants will, however, perform far better the second year after planting, once they have rooted well in and started to spread.

△ FOR A TRADITIONAL FINISH, *edge herbaceous borders with a strip of timber or with terracotta or Victorian-style rope twist tiles.*

Preparing the soil

Good soil preparation is vital before planting perennials. Once in place, these plants cover the soil all summer and it is difficult to improve the ground or tackle perennial weeds such as bindweed without damaging the border plants. Begin by completely eradicating any perennial weeds; some people like to leave the bed fallow for a season to allow this to be done thoroughly. Use a glyphosate-based weedkiller and repeat as often as necessary until no regrowth occurs. Then dig in as much well-rotted organic matter as possible. Double digging is well worth the effort, as it increases the depth of good soil available to plant roots and improves the moisture-holding capacity of the soil – this will be a great advantage in dry summers. Improve the texture of clay

◁ HERBACEOUS BORDERS *look their best in summer, when flowering plants like helenium, heuchera and achillea make a blaze of colour.*

△ IN LATE SUMMER *or autumn, when plants die back naturally, cut the old foliage and flower stems close to ground level to tidy the border.*

soil by digging in grit at the same time. Finally, rake in a dressing of general fertilizer immediately before planting.

FORMAL OR INFORMAL?

Traditional formal borders backed by hedges look impressive but are labour-intensive; the hedge can harbour pests such as slugs as well as weeds and it shades plants from one side, causing slightly leggy growth that requires more staking. Since you will need access for cutting the hedge, try to leave a path 60cm (2ft) wide between it and the back of the border from which to work – or place a few slabs along the back to use as 'stepping stones', to avoid treading on plants. Herbaceous borders generally need to be at least 90cm (3ft) wide so the plants look in scale with their surroundings. Island beds are more informal in appearance. Their advantage is that the plants are exposed to light from all sides and consequently grow tough and compact, so that only the tallest, like delphiniums, need support.

Group herbaceous plants in threes or fives of a kind so they make large clumps quickly and have more effect in a large border. In small beds a single specimen may be enough, especially of the more vigorous species. Place tall plants to the back and in the centre of a border, with the shortest at the front, creating a tiered effect that allows all the flowers to be seen properly. In informal gardens, the effect of flowers spilling over the lawn is charming, but in more formal surroundings a 'mowing strip' is an advantage. This is a row of bricks or other small paving units forming a narrow divider along the front of the border onto which the front row of plants can fall forward. This prevents them getting under the blades of a mower and also saves the grass from developing bare and yellow patches which become evident in autumn, when the plants are cut back. A mowing strip also provides a dry path from which to weed in wet weather.

△ AFTER FLOWERING *in early and mid-summer, cut* Alchemilla mollis *back close to ground level to encourage fresh, new foliage.*

CARING FOR HERBACEOUS PERENNIALS

○ Mulch flower borders in early spring when the soil is moist and weed-free, using a 2.5–5cm (1–2in) layer of well-rotted organic matter. If a dry spring is likely in your area, mulch in autumn instead.

○ Feed plants in mid-spring when some growth is above ground; prevent fertilizer lodging in the crowns of plants as it may scorch them (if this happens, flush it out with plenty of water). For peak performance, top up the nutrients every 6–8 weeks by sprinkling fertilizer between plants and hoeing it in or, if the soil is dry, by liquid feeding.

○ Support tall or floppy perennials using bushy pea-sticks, proprietary support frames or bamboo canes, according to the type of plant. Put supports in place in mid- to late spring, before the plants grow tall enough to start flopping.

○ Deadhead flowers as soon as they are over to encourage a further flush; some plants, such as lupins, pulmonaria and astrantia, are best cut down almost to ground level after flowering as this encourages a second flush of growth and possibly more flowers.

○ Tidy up dead stems and leaves in autumn, cutting them off almost to ground level and putting the plant material on the compost heap.

○ Divide large clumps of perennials every 3–5 years, discarding the woody centre of the plant and replanting the younger outer portions of it.

37

Sowing and using hardy annuals

Hardy annuals are the easiest plants to raise from seed. They need no special facilities and can be sown straight into the garden in spring, as they withstand colder conditions than bedding plants. Hardy annuals include many old-fashioned flowers, like nasturtium, calendula, cornflower, larkspur, clarkia, godetia and sweet peas, all of which characterize cottage-style gardens.

38

SOWING IN SITU

Sowing where plants are to flower is a practical option only where the soil is free from weed seeds as a result of many years' good cultivation. Otherwise, make a 'stale seedbed' by preparing the site and leaving it fallow the previous year, hoeing weekly to kill germinating weed seeds; do not turn the soil over before sowing as this would expose a new crop of weed seeds to the light, which then germinate. To achieve a traditional cottagey, Persian-carpet style annual bed, rake the soil lightly then mark out a pattern of informal shapes with the point of a stick or by trickling an outline of sand. Sow one variety in each of the shapes created, putting the tallest to the back, then rake lightly to cover the seed. Thin only if the seedlings come up too thickly.

SOWING IN ROWS FOR TRANSPLANTING

Where the soil is likely to contain weed seeds, it is safest to sow hardy annual seed in rows, so that the emerging seedlings are easy to distinguish from those of weeds. Any spare

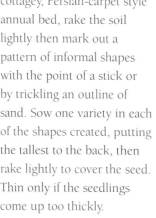

◁ **WHERE SOIL** *is well-cultivated and free from weeds, annuals sown in* situ *make a quick and easy carpet of colour; it needs little work as the closely planted annuals smother weeds.*

piece of well-cultivated ground can be used, but a vacant corner of the vegetable garden is usually most convenient. Prepare the soil as for sowing vegetables and sprinkle the seed thinly along a shallow drill. Cover thinly – on heavy clay soil or silty ground likely to cap (form a hard crust on the surface), cover the seed with compost or vermiculite, as this gives better germination. When seedlings emerge, thin to leave them about 5cm (2in) apart, and when big enough to handle easily, transplant them to their flowering

◁ **A MIXTURE OF PLANT TYPES**, *here including the feathery foliage of cosmos, makes up the traditional cottage garden border. Hardy annuals such as calendula marigolds and sunflowers will seed themselves gently around, without needing to be replanted each year.*

positions. Hardy annuals are most effective planted in groups among shrubs, or they can be massed together in flower beds.

SOWING IN TRAYS

Sometimes, perhaps due to lack of space, it is more convenient to sow hardy annuals in trays. Prepare the trays and sow in the same way as for half-hardy annual bedding plants, in early to mid-spring. But since hardy annuals need no heat, the trays can be placed in an unheated greenhouse, sunroom, enclosed porch or cold frame, or can even be stood outdoors, covered by cloches or a sheet of glass. They will germinate as soon as weather conditions are warm enough.

When the seedlings are big enough to handle, either prick them out as for bedding plants and grow them on in a cold frame, or simply thin the seedlings out to leave the remainder 5cm (2in) apart in the same tray. Plant them out when they are big enough. This method is a useful way of raising a few plants to put into containers or to fill gaps in small beds.

AUTUMN SOWING

Hardy annuals can be given an early start by sowing them in mid-autumn under cold glass. Sow several seeds per 13cm (5in) pot and allow all the seedlings to grow; this will produce a bushy plant fast. Compact varieties of nasturtium and calendula, make bright spring-flowering pot plants for a cold greenhouse. Taller varieties of annuals can be put out into the garden once the worst of the weather is over – they will provide welcome splashes of colour in the lull between the last of the spring bulbs and bedding and the first flowers of the summer bedding.

△ **SWEET PEAS** *are an old favourite hardy annual. Seeds are often sown under cold glass in autumn to give early blooms for cut flowers but spring-sown plants flower later into the summer.*

MAKING THE MOST OF HARDY ANNUALS

○ Some hardy annuals self-seed, especially nigella, alyssum, nasturtium and calendula. They rarely become a nuisance and their seedlings can create a charming, country-garden effect by appearing randomly among shrubs in borders or cracks in paving.

○ Saving your own seed is a practical proposition with hardy annuals; look out for ripening seedpods and capsules in summer and gather before the seed falls naturally. Allow the seedhead to dry thoroughly, then extract the seed and store in paper envelopes to sow in autumn or spring.

○ If sown early enough, hardy annuals will begin flowering slightly ahead of summer bedding plants. Regular feeding, watering and dead-heading help keep them flowering over the longest possible period. However, they come to an end earlier, so you should anticipate many kinds being over by midsummer. If you want some late-flowering colour, make a late sowing at the end of spring or in early summer.

○ Being rather tougher than summer bedding plants, hardy annuals are useful flowers to plant in cold locations or in containers and hanging baskets in an exposed situation. Both the canary creeper (*Tropaeolum peregrinum*) and trailing nasturtiums are especially good for hanging baskets.

39

Planting bulbs

Spring-, summer- and autumn-flowering bulbs provide the opportunity to add an extra layer of colour to the garden. Plant them under shrubs or between perennials in the flower border or use them to naturalize informally in lawns and orchards, or formally in seasonal bedding displays. And plant bulbs in pots for splashes of colour all round the garden.

△ **FOR A GOOD** *display in pots, plant two layers of bulbs, one below the other. In a big container, you could add a third tier, their tips at soil level.*

40

▽ **EARLY-FLOWERING** *spring bulbs such as winter aconites, snowdrops and Cyclamen coum make stunning carpets of colour beneath large trees, before they come into leaf.*

SOIL AND SITUATION

Bulbs need well-drained but moisture-retentive soil, containing plenty of well-rotted organic matter. Fork in a bucketful of gritty sand per square metre to improve clay soil, and plant bulbs susceptible to rotting, such as lilies, crown imperial and tulips, on a 2.5cm (1in) layer of grit placed at the bottom of the planting hole. Mix in a special bulb fertilizer or superphosphate before planting. Most bulbs need a sunny situation, though lilies like their roots shaded by surrounding plants. Dwarf narcissi, hardy cyclamen and snowdrops will thrive in light, dappled shade, for instance under trees or shrubs. As a general rule, plant bulbs at three times their own depth, using a trowel or bulb planting tool – if planted too shallowly they may not flower again for several years.

NATURALIZING IN BORDERS

Spring bulbs grown under shrubs or among perennials get borders off to an early start. Specially suitable are carpets of *Anemone blanda*, snowdrops or drifts of narcissi, especially dwarf kinds like 'February Gold' and 'Jet Fire', which have compact foliage. After flowering, allow the leaves to die down naturally; mask the untidy foliage of large narcissi by planting them towards the back of the border, with perennials in front. Space bulbs about half as far apart as the height of the flowers; this allows room for clumps to spread for several years before they get overcrowded and need lifting and dividing. Move snowdrops after flowering but while the leaves are green, other spring bulbs in late summer – mark the spot so you know where they are.

△ **SNAKE'S-HEAD FRITTILARIES,** *with their nodding, bell-shaped spring flowers in an unusual chequered pattern, are superb plants to naturalize under trees in damp soil.*

NATURALIZING IN LAWNS

To create a random effect, drop handfuls of bulbs from waist height and plant where they land. Large 'drifts' of crocus, narcissi, scilla or snowdrops look most effective; *Fritillaria meleagris* and *Anemone blanda* are very striking too. Strip back a section of turf and plant the bulbs, after improving the soil as above, then lay the turf back over the top. Do not cut the grass for at least six weeks after flowering, or until the bulb foliage has died down naturally, otherwise the following year's flowering will be impaired. Feed both grass and bulbs with a lawn feed that does not contain a herbicide in spring and autumn. Avoid planting bulbs too close to a hedge, or they will starve.

FORMAL PLANTING

Bulbs such as hyacinths and tulips, which benefit from being lifted annually and stored during the summer, are good candidates for formal bedding, though

▽ TO NATURALIZE crocus bulbs in the lawn, strip back a piece of turf, scatter the corms and plant them where they fall, then simply replace the turf over them.

other bulbs can also be used. After the summer bedding is cleared, fork superphosphate into the soil and plant spring bulbs. Plant either in rows, as edging round winter and spring bedding, or in geometric-shaped blocks. After flowering, dig bulbs out while the foliage is still green to make the beds available for summer bedding. Heel the bulbs into any spare part of the garden to complete their growth cycle; when the foliage dies down, dig them up, dry them off and store for the summer in a cool, shady shed, ready to replant in the garden in autumn.

PLANTING IN POTS

Spring bulbs such as hyacinths, tulips and dwarf narcissi make good subjects for pots, tubs, troughs and window boxes. Team them with spring bedding like wallflowers or use them alone and plant in a soil-based compost. The usual planting rules do not apply in pots: plant bulbs close enough together so they are not quite touching, and so the tips of bulbs are level with the surface of the compost. Stand containers in a cool spot for several months after planting while the bulbs form roots, taking care to avoid heavy rain and the risk of

◁ NARCISSUS POETICUS 'PLENUS' is an old cottage-garden favourite with scented flowers, ideal for planting in a lawn or on a bank.

BULBS FOR ALL SEASONS

SPRING BULBS: plant early-rooters like daffodils in early autumn; leave tulips and hyacinths till mid-autumn.

SUMMER BULBS: plant hardy kinds like nerines, galtonia and *Amaryllis belladonna* in spring and leave to naturalize in a warm, sunny spot; plant non-hardy bulbs such as tigridia, gladiolus, canna and eucomis in late spring and lift after flowering, before the first frost.

AUTUMN BULBS: autumn-flowering bulbs such as colchicum, sternbergia and autumn crocus are available for a limited time in late summer, so plant immediately: foliage does not appear until the following spring and should be left undisturbed. Plant hardy cyclamen from pots when in growth, with the tuber just above ground.

waterlogging. Move to their final positions on the patio or by the front door once the weather has turned colder. Leave pots that are to be brought indoors outside until the buds form, then keep them in a cool room.

Growing and caring for alpines

The term alpine includes dwarf bulbs, rosette plants such as sempervivums, low ground-hugging species, compact mound-shaped plants and miniature shrubs, all of which need well-drained conditions. Alpines are rarely grown, as they used to be, in rockeries, since it is undesirable to remove limestone and other rock from their natural habitats, but attractive, alternative ways of growing them include raised beds and sink gardens.

RAISED BEDS

On heavy soils, or where drainage is not very good, building a raised bed makes it easy to create conditions where surplus water can run away quickly. The walls may be made of brick, stone or walling blocks to suit the particular garden; dry stone walling gives a natural, rural look while walling blocks make a more formal effect. The bed is filled with a mixture of grit, weed-free topsoil and peat substitutes such as coir or leafmould in roughly equal proportions; this mixture gives good drainage yet retains enough moisture for alpine plants. The top of

▷ IN THIS ENTHUSIAST'S PLOT, a heavily planted raised rock feature forms a complete garden. The decorative mulch of stone chippings creates well-drained conditions for alpine plants.

a raised alpine bed is often decorated with pieces of rock and, after planting, topped with a dressing of stone chippings.

SCREE BEDS

A scree bed can be made on level ground or on a slight slope, where the soil is naturally free-draining, or it can be created in a raised bed. A garden scree bed is intended to duplicate the conditions that are found in natural scree at the foot of a mountain, where small pieces of rock debris build up. In a garden, a scree bed contains a mixture of equal parts of gravel and soil, which provides very good drainage, topped with a layer of pebbles or rock chippings, which furnish a natural-looking background for alpine plants. The sharper drainage means that choicer alpines can be grown than would survive in a normal garden bed. This type of bed can be decorated with pieces of rock too.

42

▷ IN SPRING, weed carefully between clumps of alpine plants in a raised bed and top up the layer of stone chippings or gravel. This improves surface drainage and acts as a mulch, to retain moisture and smother weeds.

YEAR-ROUND ALPINES

Given good growing conditions, alpines are very little trouble and will provide interest in the garden throughout the year.

SPRING CARE

In early spring, weed thoroughly and take precautions against slugs. The majority of alpines are spring-flowering, so rock features should look their best now. This is also a good time to add new plants to the display. After flowering, take cuttings using the soft, young shoots of the new growth. Root in pots of seed compost in a cool, shady spot protected from the weather – a well-ventilated cold frame in shade is perfect. Many alpines are best propagated regularly so that old or exhausted plants can be replaced; it is sometimes possible to detach portions of spreading species with some root to make new plants. Give a light feed during this season.

SUMMER CARE

In dry weather, even alpines may need watering, but it is best to give a thorough soaking then leave them alone – light waterings just bring roots to the surface and make plants less able to manage on their own.

AUTUMN CARE

In autumn, remove dead foliage from the plants and clear fallen leaves. Top up surface chippings, tucking them under rosette plants to help deter slugs and improve drainage round the neck of the plants – this helps to prevent rotting in winter.

WINTER CARE

Protect delicate plants from excess wet by covering them with an inclined sheet of glass to deflect rain; do not use cloches as it is essential for alpines to have plenty of fresh air.

43

MAKING A FAKE STONE SINK

❖

Real stone sinks are very expensive but ceramic sinks can be coated with a substance called hypertufa to make them resemble stone.

1 First spread outdoor adhesive over the outside of the sink to make a rough surface on to which the mixture can grip.

2 When the adhesive is dry, mix equal volumes of coarse sand, cement and coarse coir or peat to a slightly sticky paste with water. Slap it roughly over the outside of the sink by hand, wearing rubber gloves, to leave a craggy finish. Use a wire brush to contour the surface as it dries.

3 Allow several weeks for the coating to set before planting up the sink.

PLANTING UP A SINK GARDEN

❖

Sink gardens are like mini-screes or raised beds in a container. They are the perfect way to house a small collection of choice, compact alpines and make a very attractive feature for a patio. If they are raised up, they bring the plants to eye level, where their intricate beauty can be appreciated in detail.

1 Fill the sink with a mixture of one part John Innes potting compost No. 3, one part coir or leafmould and one part coarse, gritty sand.

2 Plant the sink with a varied selection of mound-shaped, rosette and creeping plants, choosing plenty of evergreens for year-round interest.

3 Decorate the surface with a 'mulch' of stone chippings and perhaps one or two small chunks of rock.

4 Despite their reputation for drought-tolerance, alpines grown in a sink garden will need to be watered during dry spells due to the restricted volume of soil in the container, which may easily dry out all too quickly.

Choosing a greenhouse

A greenhouse is the ultimate garden accessory. It allows you to raise your own plants from seeds and cuttings and to grow food crops such as tomatoes and cucumbers that do best under cover. In a heated greenhouse you can overwinter half-hardy perennials, grow and display greenhouse pot plants like cineraria, and cultivate specialist collections such as fuchsias or cacti.

TYPES OF GREENHOUSE

Greenhouses are made of metal or wood. Cedar greenhouses look best in the garden but they need regular timber treatment and are more expensive; those made of aluminium are maintenance-free. The most popular greenhouse size is 2.5m by 1.8m (8ft by 6ft) and economy models are available at DIY superstores. But you will have to go to a specialist manufacturer to supply larger sizes, unusual shapes, stronger models suitable for windy areas and greenhouses with superior glazing systems (best if you plan to heat). Round greenhouses take up least room but offer a large growing area for plants; lean-to greenhouses make use of a house wall and trap heat better than freestanding models.

44

△ A VICTORIAN-STYLE *greenhouse makes a feature in the garden. This model has ventilators running the length of the ridge, which helps to keep temperatures down in summer.*

◁ ALTHOUGH WOODEN *greenhouses need regular timber treatment, their advantage is that you can easily fasten bubble wrap or shading fabric onto them using nothing more than drawing pins.*

OPTIONAL EXTRAS

❖

- An electric propagating case is the most economical way to maintain a high temperature in a small area: use for propagating plants in spring or autumn, and for overwintering small, delicate plants that need a higher temperature than the rest of the greenhouse.

- An automatic watering system is a great time-saver: main feeder tubes run along staging or the border, from which micro-tubes drip water on to individual plants. The system may be supplied from a container of water in the greenhouse or the mains tap. A 'computer' can be added to time waterings automatically.

EQUIPPING THE GREENHOUSE

Fit automatic ventilator openers to prevent the greenhouse overheating if you are away from home during the day; extra ventilators or a louvred vent in the back wall of the house are also useful. You can install blinds to help keep the temperature down, though this can also be achieved by painting the outside of the glass with liquid shading in summer. You will need staging to grow pot plants or to care for seedlings in trays; two-tier staging doubles the available growing space. Most owners have staging down one side of the house and

▷ IN SPRING, *greenhouse space is at a premium when seed sowing and plant potting are under way. Staging makes the best use of heated space.*

leave a soil border on the other; crops like tomatoes are best grown in the ground. A paved floor provides a firm base for staging and makes it easy to keep the greenhouse clean.

HEATING

Heating allows the greenhouse to be used to the full all year round. Electricity is the best means, provided the greenhouse is within comfortable distance of the house, as it can be accurately controlled by thermostat to avoid wastage, and there is nothing to refill. Employ a contractor to lay on the supply, using armoured cable buried deep underground, and have an RCD (residual current device) built in to cut off the power in the event of accident. Alternatively, use a modern bottled gas heater with a thermostat. Aim to give just enough heat to keep the greenhouse frost-free, setting the thermostats to 5°C (40°F), to reduce electricity bills while keeping plants happy.

SPRING MAINTENANCE
- Water plants and seedlings lightly at first, increasing the frequency as the season progresses.
- Begin liquid feeding once the plants start to grow at a faster rate.
- Ventilate when the weather is warm.
- Clean the propagator and place clean silver sand in the base of it; begin seed sowing.
- In late spring, prick out seedlings and pot up rooted cuttings, re-potting any plants that need it.

SUMMER MAINTENANCE
- Water daily; stand plants on damp capillary matting spread over the tops of staging to help keep compost moist. Liquid-feed the pots regularly.
- Put up shading to help keep temperatures down.
- Take precautions against pests such as aphids and whitefly.

AUTUMN MAINTENANCE
- Reduce watering as plant growth slows down; remove capillary matting from staging and hand-water pots individually. Water in the morning so plants are not left wet overnight – damp, cool air encourages the spread of fungal diseases.
- Remove shading and, on a fine day, take everything out of the greenhouse and wash down the inside with warm water and greenhouse disinfectant, cleaning the glass and staging thoroughly.
- Put up insulation such as bubble plastic over the inner roof and walls. Return plants inside and bring tender plants under cover too.
- Turn greenhouse heating on.

WINTER MAINTENANCE
- Keep watering to a minimum; ventilate when the weather permits.
- Check that an adequate temperature is being maintained by using a max-min thermometer.

45

Using a greenhouse

Given careful management, it is possible to grow many different kinds of plants together, including food crops and ornamental pot plants, as well as raising plants from seeds and cuttings. Never be tempted to overfill the greenhouse, however; pests and diseases spread fast and are hard to tackle in overcrowded conditions, and the plants tend to grow tall and leggy.

GROWING FOOD CROPS

Vegetables that enjoy warm conditions, such as tomatoes, peppers, aubergines and cucumbers, can be grown in borders in the greenhouse during the summer months. They should be harvested and cleared away by early autumn to make room for plants needing frost protection being brought in from outside. Use the border soil in winter to grow spring onions and lettuce for out-of-season salads.

GROWING ORNAMENTALS

Tiered staging is an ideal way to display mixed summer collections of coleus, tuberous begonia, browallia, abutilon, clivia, heliotrope, gerbera and large-flowered fuchsia or petunia which would be spoiled by weather outdoors. For flowering displays in winter use indoor azalea, cyclamen, cineraria, *Primula obconica* and *P. malacoides*. Train tender climbers such as bougainvillea, plumbago, passion flower or hoya up the walls.

OVERWINTERING

Half-hardy perennials used for outdoor displays in summer, such as fuchsia, pelargonium, felicia and scaveola, can be overwintered in a frost-free greenhouse. Take cuttings in late summer, root them into trays or small pots and pot up in spring. Alternatively, dig up the plants in early autumn, cut back to a few centimetres/inches and pot up. A frost-free greenhouse is also the ideal place to house slightly tender patio shrubs, such as cordyline palms.

◁ USE POTS OF *ornamental plants like fuchsia and begonia to add a colourful edging to a greenhouse border planted with food crops. Keep pests under control – whitefly can be a nuisance.*

WINTER AND EARLY SPRING DISPLAYS

After clearing away summer crops such as tomatoes, a cold greenhouse can be used through the winter to house a range of plants. Pot-grown Christmas rose (*Helleborus niger*) and camellias flower earlier inside and their blooms cannot be spoilt by wind or sharp frosts. Use ivies with coloured primulas, ranunculus, polyanthus and early spring bulbs to create a colourful display on the staging. You can also grow hardy annual flowers in pots or collect the

46

◁ AN ENTHUSIAST'S *greenhouse, set up specially for cultivating tender plants. Note the max-min thermometer for checking the correct temperature is maintained at all times. The floor has been damped down for extra humidity.*

∇ WHEN HEATED *greenhouse space is available, make full use of it for propagating your own plants. Cuttings rooted in late summer occupy little bench space in winter.*

47

earliest-flowering alpines, such as many saxifrages and dwarf bulbs. Use the roof space for overwintering pelargoniums in hanging baskets or plant baskets up in early spring and suspend them from the greenhouse roof until the frosts are over.

GROWING SPRING BULBS IN POTS
Choose firm, plump, healthy bulbs. Plant them so that their 'noses' are just showing (there is no need to plant them at the same depth as you would in the ground) and close together, almost touching, for a good display. Water

lightly, then place in a cool, dark place so the bulbs can form roots: use a shed, garage or the space beneath an oil tank; if it is warm, shoots will appear too soon.

When the leaves appear, move into a cold or frost-free greenhouse, keeping them in light shade for a few days to accustom them to the light gradually. Give just enough water to keep the compost moist, without making it too wet; feed fortnightly with weak liquid tomato feed. After flowering, tip the bulbs out of their pots and plant the entire clump in the garden.

SPECIALIST COLLECTIONS
❖

After cultivating a mixed collection of plants, many greenhouse gardeners develop a taste for one particular group of plants – perhaps cacti, fuchsias, pelargoniums or giant-flowered exhibition begonias – and wish to specialize in them. You can then set up the greenhouse to cater to their needs, perhaps buying specialist equipment like blinds, heaters or fans.

Pond care

Ponds provide a soothing environment for people and a valuable habitat for garden wildlife. They also present a unique opportunity to grow a fascinating range of plants that could not easily be accommodated elsewhere. Ponds need regular maintenance to keep them looking their best.

48

◁ **DUCKWEED** *consists of two tiny leaves that float on the water's surface, with short, trailing roots. It multiplies rapidly, forming mats that smother the pond. Skim them off with a fish net.*

INTRODUCING PLANTS

The start of the growing season is the time to add new plants to the pond. Most 'marginal' plants such as water iris (*Iris laevigata*), marsh marigold (*Caltha palustris*) and pickerel weed (*Pontederia cordata*) need positioning so they have 7.5cm (3in) of water over the top of their pots. Stand them on shallow planting shelves round the edge of the pond. Water lilies need deeper water, 15–45cm (6–18in) depending on the variety. Large varieties are in any case too invasive for normal garden ponds; choose dwarf kinds, which also prefer shallow water.

Always buy water plants grown in baskets, and sink them into the pond slowly; stand them on bricks if needed to achieve the correct depth. Floating aquatics such as water lettuce, water hyacinth or water chestnut add variety but are not winter-hardy, so they will need to be re-introduced annually.

It is essential to include oxygenating plants (submerged water weeds) if you keep fish in the pond; they are not grown in baskets, but root themselves into the silt at the bottom of the pond. Canadian pondweed is the most popular kind; being evergreen, it releases oxygen into the water even in winter, besides providing shelter for fish.

DIVIDING WATER PLANTS

Established water plants will need dividing every few years, when they become congested. Lift the planting baskets out of the pond and remove the old plants. Divide in the same way as for garden perennials, then discard the old growth from the centre of the clump and replant one healthy division taken from the edge. Line the basket with hessian or with fine plastic mesh sold for this purpose, then fill with special aquatic compost or ordinary soil that has not been treated with fertilizer. Put pebbles on top of the compost to weigh it down, and replace the basket carefully in the pond.

◁ **A FOUNTAIN** *brings the sound of moving water to a garden. Variegated iris are good plants for small ponds and enjoy being splashed by water.*

△ CANADIAN PONDWEED *is a vigorous and invasive water plant but it is the only one that is evergreen and does not die off in winter. It is therefore an essential ingredient to keep water oxygenated if you have fish. Thin out excess growth several times during the summer.*

DEALING WITH MURKY WATER

Green or murky water is a common problem with new ponds and often also affects established ponds temporarily in spring while aquatic organisms reach their own balance. The problem normally resolves itself within a few months. It helps to keep the water clear if you use a mixture of marginals and enough water lilies or other floating plants to shade half the water surface. A small underwater pump will also help clear murky ponds by aerating the water and filters can remove some algae. A wad of organically grown barley straw sunk in the water sometimes keeps the water clear as will chemical products, available from garden centres or aquatic suppliers.

BLANKET WEED

❖

Blanket weed is a type of algae, forming fibrous strands that build up into thick, cottonwool-like masses, choking the pond. It is liable to get out of control where nitrogen fertilizer leaches into the pond from the surrounding garden and where there are too few marginal and other pond plants. Remove blanket weed regularly by hand or insert the tip of a cane into the mass, twirl it round and lift out. If removed often enough, blanket weed slowly reduces the nitrogen levels in a pond and the growth of weed becomes less of a problem. It makes a good compost ingredient.

◁ TOP UP THE *water level of ponds weekly in summer. If you see fish gasping at the surface in hot weather, this indicates oxygen shortage. Spray the water surface with a fine shower from the hose as this gets air into the water fast.*

SUMMER CARE
○ All forms of water weed spread rapidly and will need regular thinning in summer: simply pull out handfuls, shaking out fish fry and tadpoles. Put waste weed on the compost heap.

○ When working in the garden, take care not to allow fertilizers or chemicals in or near the pond as these can kill fish or encourage the growth of algae.

○ In hot weather, top ponds up regularly with ordinary tap water – water levels can drop 2.5–5cm (1–2in) per week. (If this happens all year round, you should suspect a leaking pond liner.)

○ Leave a pump running to add extra oxygen to the water in summer, as fish tend to suffer in hot weather.

49

AUTUMN/WINTER CARE
○ Stop feeding fish once the weather turns cooler and they become less active, otherwise unused food will decompose and pollute the pond.

○ Remove dead or dying foliage from marginal plants and take out floating aquatics, such as water hyacinth, that are not frost-hardy. These can be over-wintered in jars of pond water on a bright windowsill indoors, or discarded.

○ Cover the pond with netting to prevent fallen leaves contaminating the pond and to keep out herons, which take fish from garden ponds in winter. Clear dead leaves from the netting frequently.

Growing in containers

Containers filled with tender plants make eye-catching displays on a patio. But tubs, pots and troughs are also a convenient way to grow plants in all sorts of situations where there is no soil, turning paved courtyards, terraces and even steps into oases of colour. The beauty of containers is that they are mobile so you can move them to wherever some interest or a splash of colour is needed.

△ **MAKE THE MOST OF** *containers to create a garden in places that are totally without soil. Mix tall pots with hanging baskets and pots on plinths.*

TYPES OF CONTAINER

Terracotta pots are the traditional favourite and come in all shapes and sizes but, being porous, the plants in them dry out fast. Frostproof terracotta is less likely to crack if used outside in winter. Glazed ceramic pots, some decorated with oriental designs, are colourful and look especially good teamed with flowers that coordinate with the pot colour. Plastic containers are the most economical; cheap plastic becomes brittle when exposed to sunlight over several years, but the high-quality ones are more durable. Wooden containers such as tubs or half barrels last longest if lined with black polythene before use – be sure to cut matching drainage holes in the plastic liner.

POTTING COMPOST

You can use any type of potting compost in containers. Soil-based kinds are heavier, so they provide greater stability for tall or top-heavy plants, whereas on a roof garden, where weight is a consideration, you would

△ **PLANT POTS,** *planters and troughs can be bought in plastic, terracotta, timber and ceramic in an immense range of styles, shapes and sizes. Avoid mixing too many different kinds together as the effect will be bitty.*

▽ **IN A LARGE** *container, you can almost create a potted flower bed; pack in the plants for best display.*

SUMMER CARE

DRYING OUT is the biggest risk for plants in containers, so check regularly and water as often as necessary to keep the compost moist. In midsummer, watering may be needed daily – twice daily for small containers – but take care not to overwater at the start of the season, while growth is slow.

FEED CONTAINERS once a week from late spring to late summer. Liquid tomato feed is ideal for any flowering plants: dilute to half or quarter normal strength, depending on plant vigour. This can be used in addition to slow-release fertilizer for real show-stopping displays.

DEAD-HEADING is vital for plants grown in containers, as they are on show all the time. Do this twice weekly all summer to keep plants tidy and flowering well.

PLANTING UP CONTAINERS

1 Cover large drainage holes in the base of the container with crocks or polystyrene pieces to stop the compost trickling out.

2 Part-fill the container with compost, leaving plenty of room for the plant rootballs.

3 Having watered the plants, knock them out of their containers, tapping the rim down firmly on a hard surface to loosen them. If badly pot-bound, gently tease out some of the largest roots.

4 Arrange the plants in position and fill round the rootballs with more compost, firming them gently in place. Keep the final level of compost well below the pot rim to make watering easier.

5 Water well, push in any plant supports that may be needed, and move the container to its final position.

51

do better to use a soilless compost. To make the routine care of container plants easier, mix water-retaining gel crystals and slow-release fertilizer granules into the compost before planting up, following the maker's instructions carefully.

SUMMER PLANTS FOR CONTAINERS

Containers for summer displays may be planted after the last frost or, if you have space in a frost-free greenhouse, they can be planted up to six weeks earlier and displays allowed to mature before they can safely be put outside. Use any reasonably compact kinds of bedding plant or half-hardy perennials such as fuchsia, pelargonium, gazania or felicia. A combination of trailing plants, such as lobelia, with upright plants like begonia and bushy subjects like pelargonium, makes a good display. Group several similar pots together and follow a distinct planting theme to create an eye-catching container garden.

WINTER AND SPRING DISPLAYS

When the summer bedding is over, shortly before the first frosts, empty and replant containers for winter and spring colour. There is no need to replace the compost as winter plants prefer it low in nutrients. Remove all spent plants and their roots, and if necessary top up the container with more compost. Replant with spring bulbs, winter-flowering pansies, or spring bedding such as polyanthus, primulas or wallflowers. Foliage plants like ivies or euonymus can be added as fillers. Alternatively, to avoid the risk of plants being damaged during a severe winter, you can wait until spring; buy spring bedding such as ranunculus or forget-me-nots and plant into containers when already flowering for immediate impact.

Place winter and spring containers in a sheltered spot and prevent any waterlogging by raising them up on bricks or pot feet. In early summer, when winter and spring flowers are over, remove the plants and completely replace the compost, ready for summer bedding.

Year-round containers

Bedding plants need replacing in summer and autumn to keep containers colourful all year round but hardy evergreen plants make ideal permanent candidates for containers. Choose compact kinds of shrub, conifer, ivy, phormium and hardy palms for best effect. Some deciduous plants, such as hostas and clematis, also make excellent container subjects.

POTS AND POTTING COMPOST

Instead of growing a mixture of plants in a single container, as with summer schemes, use only one specimen shrub per large pot for year-round interest or plant a group of herbaceous plants such as hostas in a wide container. Plastic or wooden containers are most durable for outdoor use in winter; if using terracotta or ceramic pots, choose frost-resistant kinds to prevent cracking in cold weather (contrary to popular belief, they do not protect the plants in them from freezing).

Soil-based composts are the most suitable for plants that will remain in the same pots for several years as they retain nutrients better than peat- or coir-based mixes. If you are growing lime-hating plants, such as azaleas or camellias, use ericaceous compost. Add water-retaining gel crystals and slow-release fertilizer to the compost when planting up; reapply the fertilizer every spring by making holes in the compost with a pencil and trickling it down.

52

WINTER CARE
❖

- Containers may need occasional watering even in winter since walls and fences often deflect rainfall.

- Raise pots up on bricks or 'pot feet' to prevent waterlogging.

- Avoid feeding after late summer as this would encourage soft growth, easily killed by frost.

- Shrubs left outside for winter may need tying to trellis for stability in windy weather.

- During prolonged frosty conditions it is vital to prevent containers from freezing solid as this can kill plant roots. Either lag pots with insulating material such as bubble plastic or plunge them up to their rims in garden soil and loosely drape plants with horticultural fleece. If space is available in a greenhouse, sunroom or enclosed porch, plants will be safe there. Do not leave them for more than a few days in a dark shed, however.

AUTOMATIC WATERING SYSTEMS
❖

To care for containers more easily, consider installing an irrigation system. The type of scheme employed in a greenhouse, whereby each pot is provided with its own drip pipe, can be used out of doors, with pots either connected to a water butt or linked by hose to a mains tap. If these are left in place all the time, watering can be done at the turn of a tap – or you can install a water computer to switch on and off for you. The advantage of this system is that you do not need to make any special arrangements at holiday times.

◁ **A PAIR OF** *potted evergreens either side of the door provides a formal year-round welcome, while flowering shrubs like the witch hazel* (Hamamelis mollis) *create a seasonal display.*

△ **FOR A SHADY SPOT,** Fatsia japonica *and ivies make a good container team. The fatsia flowers in winter, when little else is in bloom.*

MATURE CONTAINERS

Most slow-growing plants can be left in the same container for three to five years before they need repotting, provided they are in soil-based compost and receive regular feeding. Simply remove the top layer of compost every spring and replace it with fresh (this also removes any moss or liverwort that may be growing on the surface of the compost). If plants outgrow their container or their growth declines, you will need to repot them sooner. For most plants, the best time to do this is spring, at the start of the growing season, although spring-flowering plants such as dwarf rhododendron are best left until immediately after flowering. Carefully remove plants (if they are too big for the container, plant them out in the garden), refill the tub with fresh compost and replant with either the original plants or with new ones.

▷ **EXOTIC PLANTS** *like agave and Chusan palm* (Trachycarpus fortunei) *can be grown outside in summer (in very mild regions, all year round). If frost threatens, bring the pots under cover.*

PERMANENT PLANT SUBJECTS

Compact evergreen shrubs such as hebe, euonymus, choisya and rosemary make ideal subjects for large containers or you can use potted topiary specimens clipped from bay or box. Architectural plants such as *Fatsia japonica* and phormium look especially striking when isolated in pots and in mild areas you can use slightly tender, architectural evergreens like the Chusan palm (*Trachycarpus fortunei*) and cordylines, as they will survive outside in winter. Lime-hating shrubs such as dwarf rhododendrons, camellia and pieris make good tub specimens and, where the garden soil is unsuitable, this is often the only way to grow them, using ericaceous compost. Some striking deciduous plants are perfect for pots, including Japanese maple, hostas (which are easier to protect from slugs in pots), heucheras and clematis grown up obelisks. Shade clematis by growing other plants around the pot, to keep their roots cool and moist. Conifers also look good in containers, provided they can be prevented from drying out: if this happens their foliage goes brown and does not recover.

◁ **IN A SUDDEN** *frost, use old newspapers for emergency lagging. Once compost freezes solid, plant roots are unable to take up moisture and even the hardiest plants can die.*

53

Growing in hanging baskets

Hanging baskets are the perfect way to display trailing plants and to bring a splash of colour to walls, doorways and porches. You can follow a display of summer annuals by winter and spring bedding. As they are surrounded by air on all sides, baskets tend to dry out quickly, but hanging them in a sheltered spot and giving them frequent attention are the secrets of success.

△ **VARIEGATED HEBE,** *trailing ivies and winter pansies form the basis of a winter basket.*

54

TYPES OF BASKET

Traditional wire baskets look wonderful, although their open-weave sides mean that the contents dry out fast; when the compost is bone dry, water runs straight through, making it difficult to wet again. Wire baskets need to be lined before they can hold compost; moss is the favourite material as plants can still be grown through the sides of the basket. Various flexible fabric or plastic linings can be bought and black polythene can also be used, though these are less natural looking: cut holes in the sides for planting through. Solid-sided hanging baskets are also available, made of plastic, terracotta or ceramic, some with built-in water reservoirs. Though easier to look after, they can only be planted at the top.

THE BEST PLANTS

Trailing plants such as lobelia, petunia, ivy-leaved pelargonium and trailing fuchsia make the most obvious candidates but plants with a naturally lax, bushy habit, like impatiens, laurentia and brachycome also look good in hanging baskets. Annual climbers such as *Thunbergia alata*, morning glory (*Ipomoea*) and dwarf sweet peas make good basket subjects too; tie some stems round the sides, leaving others to climb up the supporting chains.

WINTER AND EARLY SPRING BASKETS

These only succeed in a really well-sheltered spot or if baskets can be moved under cover in bad weather. After summer flowers are over, empty

◁ **AS SUMMER BASKETS** *have a long growing season, you can cultivate sensational displays like this. The secret lies in starting early, with good plants, then keeping them well-fed, watered and regularly dead-headed. Choose old favourites like fuchsia, petunia and pelargonium for a prolific display.*

the basket and replant with winter-flowering pansies or, for a more weatherproof scheme, a mixture of ivies, winter-flowering heathers, euonymus and santolina; dwarf bulbs like crocus, iris or daffodil can be included. If you wait until spring you can plant primroses, violas or polyanthus in flower, with ivies for foliage 'trails'.

EDIBLE BASKETS

A hanging basket by the back door makes a handy place to grow herbs or a mixture of salad leaves such as sorrel, purslane, American land cress, rocket and cut-and-come-again lettuces. Or choose compact, trailing varieties of tomato, miniature cucumber or strawberry, giving each crop its own basket. Watering and feeding are crucial, but slugs are less of a problem than at ground level, and crops can easily be protected from birds by draping with netting or a crop-protection fleece.

△ FOR A SOPHISTICATED *scheme, go for plenty of coloured foliage with hints of flower. This basket holds coleus, helichrysum,* Heuchera *'Palace Purple' and* Verbena *'Peaches and Cream'.*

ROUTINE BASKET CARE

❖

- Watering: check hanging baskets daily, and give enough water to keep the compost moist. In summer, when the basket is full of roots, water both morning and evening.

- If wire baskets get so dry that water runs through them, lift down and soak in a bowl of water overnight.

- Special pulley devices are available to make watering easier by lowering the baskets for watering, as well as extension arms for hoses that reach up into high baskets.

- Feeding: regular feeding is vital to keep plants growing and flowering well in a small amount of compost. Use high-potash liquid tomato feed once or twice a week; apply at half strength until plants fill the basket.

55

PLANTING A LINED WIRE BASKET

❖

1 *Place the fibre liner inside the basket and cut to size if it overlaps round the edge. Part-fill with potting compost mixed with water-retaining gel crystals and slow-release fertilizer granules. Push small plants in through the overlapping sections of the liner, so they make a ring halfway up the basket sides. (Or line the basket with wads of moss.)*

2 *Fill the basket to the rim with more compost, firming lightly to settle it round the roots of the first row of plants. Then plant a second layer in the overlapping sections of the liner, pushing the plants in from the outside of the basket. Choose plants that contrast in form and colour with the previous ones for a more interesting display.*

3 *Finally, plant the top of the basket; you could either use more bedding plants or choose climbers or, as in this case, a single, large plant, which will form a striking centrepiece when the plants round the sides grow up to fill out the arrangement. Water well and hang in position. You could sink a plastic-bottle 'funnel' in the middle for easier watering.*

Raising plants from seed

Growing your own plants from seed is extremely satisfying and one of the cheapest ways to add new stock to the garden. No special equipment is needed – you can even use a windowsill indoors – but, as you become more adventurous, you will find that a heated electric propagator in the greenhouse provides perfect conditions for growing more challenging plants or for producing seedlings in quantity.

PROVIDING THE RIGHT CONDITIONS

56

Check the back of the seed packet or a leaflet on germination requirements (available free with your order from some mail-order seed firms) for precise instructions about individual seeds. Seeds vary mainly in the optimum temperature for their germination; plan sowings so that those needing similar heat go into the propagator together.

SOWING TIPS

❖

- Never let seeds dry out after sowing; if partly germinated, this can kill the embryo and the seeds will never come up.

- Storing seed: keep unopened packets in a cool, dry place out of direct light – do not leave in the greenhouse. Fold over the top of part-used packets and reseal with tape; put in an airtight container with a sachet of silica gel crystals. Keep in a cool place, like a refrigerator.

Some seeds, such as lettuce, require light to germinate, in which case do not put these in an airing cupboard and cover them thinly with vermiculite instead of seed compost. Other seed, such as primula, must be kept continuously moist and fail if allowed to dry out at all: it can be helpful to stand these on moist capillary matting.

SOWING SEED

Have clean trays and pots and a fresh bag of seed compost ready. Use 8cm (3½in) pots for small quantities of seed and half trays for larger amounts; square pots make the best use of propagator space. Fill them loosely with compost then level the top by running a flat-edged wooden block over it. Tap the container down gently to consolidate the compost and firm lightly with a presser. Water thoroughly and allow to drain. If sowing very fine, dust-like seed, sprinkle a thin layer of vermiculite over the surface of the compost and sprinkle

△ **A COLD FRAME** is *a useful extra alongside a greenhouse for hardening off all kinds of frost-tender plants for a few weeks before they can be safely planted outside.*

△ **SOW SEEDS VERY THINLY** *over the surface of the prepared seed tray. Overcrowded seedlings are more likely to succumb to fungal infections and in any case will be drawn up and leggy. You could mix seed with silver sand first.*

the seed thinly over it – there is no need to cover them. For medium-sized seeds, such as lettuce or tomato, sprinkle thinly and barely cover with sifted seed compost or vermiculite. Put on a propagating case lid, specially made to fit over a standard seed tray.

△ **PRICK OUT** *seedlings when big enough to handle but before they grow enough to get tangled together. Prick them into fresh trays of compost, spacing them about 2.5cm (1in) apart. Pot up singly when they fill the tray with roots.*

Space out larger seed like peas or beans 2.5cm (1in) or more apart and push into the compost till just buried. Large seed can also be sown singly in small, individual pots.

PRICKING OUT
When seedlings are large enough to handle (usually when the first true leaf unfolds, after the initial pair of seed leaves), loosen their roots using a pencil point or dibber and lift them out carefully. Handle the seedlings by their leaves, not by the stem – if this is bruised, a seedling often dies. Space seedlings out into trays of fresh seed compost, 2.5cm (1in) or more apart, depending on their vigour. Large seedlings are best transferred into small, individual pots at this stage.

Return freshly pricked out seedlings to the propagator or other warm, enclosed conditions out of direct sun and accustom them gradually to cooler conditions.

GROWING ON YOUNG PLANTS
Once the seedlings are established in trays or small pots, stand them on the greenhouse staging to grow until they are big enough to plant out. If you stand them on capillary matting, by simply wetting the matting regularly the containers will stay evenly moist without being over-watered. After four weeks, the nutrients in the original seed compost will be exhausted, so start weekly liquid feeding as well, using a small can. Never leave feed on the foliage as young plants may scorch. Protect from slugs and other pests, and ensure plenty of ventilation whenever possible to prevent fungal disease. Keep

the plants in good light, but shaded from strong, direct sunlight.

HARDENING OFF
Before planting outdoors, all plants – not just tender ones – need to be hardened off to accustom them gradually to lower temperatures and fluctuating outdoor conditions. To do this, stand the plants outdoors on fine days, bringing them in at night, then start leaving them out on cooler or breezier days as well, until after two to three weeks they are ready to be planted outside. If you have a cold frame, move plants from the greenhouse to the cold frame, leaving the lid on at first but start opening the lid on fine days until eventually it is left off all the time. Begin hardening off frost-tender bedding and vegetables like sweetcorn three weeks before the last expected frost, and do not plant out until after that date.

57

▽ **HARDY ANNUALS** *and vegetable seedlings like lettuces and cabbages can be sown in mid-spring and raised entirely in an unheated cold frame.*

Propagating by cuttings

Rooting cuttings is the fastest way to grow plants for the garden, provided you have access to suitable parent plants. Use this method to increase the stock of favourite plants in your own garden, to root tender perennials for overwintering and to obtain new plants from those in friends' gardens.

△ **PUT A PLASTIC** *bottle or bag over the top to maintain humidity round the cuttings, unless you are using succulent, furry or silver-leaved plants that prefer dry air.*

58

SOFTWOOD CUTTINGS

This type of cutting can be made at any time during the growing season from the soft tips of new shoots. It is best to take them near the start of the growing season, in early summer when the new shoots are young, although they are also used in late summer to propagate half-hardy perennials for overwintering as rooted cuttings.

SEMI-RIPE CUTTINGS

Often known as heel cuttings, these are taken by twisting or tearing a complete young side shoot away from the parent plant, which often leaves a small 'heel' of skin at the base of the cutting. The very base of the cutting has a small amount of slightly woody tissue, darker in colour

than the soft tissue at the tip of the shoot. Tidy the base with a sharp knife, removing torn skin and cutting cleanly below a leaf joint at the very base of the stem, leaving the woody tissue intact. About 10cm (4in) up from this, cut the tip of the shoot off just above a leaf joint. Take semi-ripe cuttings from midsummer onwards, when the plants have had time to grow side shoots.

BASAL CUTTINGS

These are commonly used to propagate herbaceous plants in spring. When new shoots appear from the crown of the plant, wait till they are a few centimetres

△ **HARDWOOD CUTTINGS** *need no special facilities: simply put prepared cuttings into a slit trench made by pushing a spade back and forth in deeply cultivated soil containing plenty of fine organic matter to create a V-shape. Firm them in using your heel along each side of the row.*

◁ **TO MAKE** *a softwood cutting, cut 10cm (4in) from the tip of a young shoot, remove the leaves from the bottom half of the shoot and cut off cleanly just below a leaf joint, using a sharp knife. Dip the cut end in hormone rooting powder, then push each cutting into a pot of seed compost and water in.*

△ JERUSALEM SAGE *(Phlomis fruticosa) roots easily from any type of cutting; for quickest results, take softwood cuttings in midsummer and root in a pot on a shady windowsill indoors.*

rooting powder specially formulated for hardwood cuttings. Make a slit trench in a well-cultivated but vacant area of the garden (such as a corner of the vegetable plot) and, if the soil is heavy, trickle 2.5cm (1in) of sharp sand into the bottom. Push the cuttings in vertically, 30cm (12in) apart, and firm the soil back round them, closing the trench. Water in. Expect them to take a year to root well enough to be moved.

high, then cut shoots 7.5–10cm (3–4in) long. The base of the cuttings will usually be pale-coloured, where light has been kept from the stem by the mulch, by nearby shoots or by the remains of last year's stems. Then treat as for softwood cuttings. Sometimes, entire shoots can be detached from the parent plant with a few small roots already formed; known as 'Irishman's cuttings', these can be potted singly but treat them as cuttings until they are well rooted.

LEAF CUTTINGS

The leaves of some stemless house plants, including African violet, *Begonia rex* and streptocarpus, can be rooted. Remove a whole leaf, complete with leaf stalk, choosing one that is young but full-sized. Push the leaf stalk into a pot of seed compost till the leaf rests on the top.

When rooted, a cluster of young plants forms at the base of the leaf. When these are about 2.5cm (1in) high, tip them out of the pot, divide them up and pot singly. The leaves of *Begonia rex* can also be laid flat on a tray of compost, with the veins in the back nicked in several places and the leaf staked to the compost with cocktail sticks. If kept humid, a young plant will form at each nick.

HARDWOOD CUTTINGS

Use this method in late autumn to propagate shrubs such as roses, willows, philadelphus, weigelas and dogwoods. Cut woody shoots from the base of the current year's growth, trim cleanly below a leaf joint (only the scar will be visible) and remove the tip to leave the cuttings 20–30cm (8–12in) long. Dip the base into a hormone

59

SUITABLE PLANTS FOR CUTTINGS

❖

The most successful plants from cuttings are soft, branching kinds that root easily. Shrubs such as magnolia and rhododendron that are expensive to buy rarely root well from cuttings and need specialist nursery equipment, hence their high price. Trees, including fruit trees, as well as bulbs, ferns and grasses are propagated by other methods; cuttings do not work. The type of cutting you take depends on the time of year and the sort of plant to be propagated.

SOFTWOOD CUTTINGS: half-hardy perennials such as pelargonium, fuchsia, osteospermum and felicia; taken during the growing season.

SEMI-RIPE CUTTINGS: shrubs like box, evergreen herbs like rosemary and soft fruit; taken in late summer.

HARDWOOD CUTTINGS: roses and easily rooted shrubs like philadelphus, cornus and ribes; taken in late autumn/early winter.

Other means of propagation

There are several ways of propagating plants other than by seed and cuttings. Subjects that have a clump-forming habit are best divided, which gives several new plants straight away. Plants that naturally produce offsets or runners grow their own rooted 'pups', which need only to be potted when they are big enough to move. And for some difficult plants that need special facilities to root from cuttings, layering is the simple alternative.

DIVISION

Dividing clumps is the fastest way to propagate plants like grasses and bamboos, herbaceous perennials including hostas and hardy cranesbills, and some house plants such as maidenhair fern. The safest time to divide most subjects is in spring, at the start of the growing season, when the new plants can start growing away at once. Tough perennials like Michaelmas daisies can, however, be divided in autumn and bearded iris should be divided six weeks after flowering.

To divide a plant, knock it out of its pot or dig it up from the garden, and separate it into several smaller clumps. Prise the roots apart by hand, or use a knife or spade. Throw away the old woody material from the centre of the clump and replant the healthy young divisions from round the edge, after improving the soil in which they are to grow with organic matter and fertilizer.

OFFSETS

Plants such as aloes, bromeliads and agaves naturally surround mature plants with small replicas of themselves, which grow from underground shoots or leaf axils. When offsets are recognizable as independent young plants with expanded foliage, the best way of removing them is to dig up the plant, or remove it from its pot, and separate the offsets carefully with your fingers, along with as much of their own roots as possible. Then pot them singly. Some plants, such as tolmeia, produce offsets from the leaves of the adult plant; in this case, wait until they grow roots naturally then pot them up, or alternatively peg a leaf down to a pot of compost while still attached to the parent; separate only when well rooted.

RUNNERS

Some plants, such as strawberries, produce runners that are rather like horizontal stems with baby plants

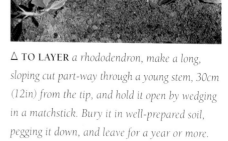

△ **TO LAYER** *a rhododendron, make a long, sloping cut part-way through a young stem, 30cm (12in) from the tip, and hold it open by wedging in a matchstick. Bury it in well-prepared soil, pegging it down, and leave for a year or more.*

growing at the end of them. These 'pups' root naturally where they are deposited by the extending runner, and in time form a large mat round the parent plant. Individual, rooted runners can be dug up and transplanted; however, in the case of strawberries, it is best to sink pots of seed compost alongside the parent plants and peg runners into them using wire hoops, so that the young plantlets root into the pots. When they are well-rooted, detach them from the parent and grow them on separately until they are big enough for planting.

△ **HARDY CRANESBILLS** *like this* Geranium *'Johnson's Blue' are quickly propagated by digging up and dividing the parent plant in early spring.*

60

△ MOST HERBACEOUS PLANTS *spread slowly to form clumps but after three to five years start to die in the middle. This is the time to dig them up and divide them, replanting only the youngest pieces.*

> ### AFTERCARE FOR NEW PLANTS
> ❖
>
> - Keep young plants out of direct sun, in humid air and at an even temperature, watering them only lightly for a week or two after propagating so that they acclimatize gradually to their new conditions.
>
> - Nip out the growing tips of young plants when potting them to encourage bushy growth.
>
> - Start feeding newly propagated plants four to six weeks after potting, as all the nutrients in the compost will then be exhausted.

LAYERING

This is the best means of propagating camellia, rhododendron, magnolia and similar plants that do not root well from cuttings. It can be done at any time of year except winter, though spring is the best season. Choose a flexible, young branch that can be pulled or bent down to ground level, and prepare the soil where it touches the ground by digging in sharp sand and well-rotted organic matter. Make a long, sloping cut towards the shoot tip, going only about a third of the way through the stem, at a convenient point in the underside of the branch, and wedge the cut open with a matchstick. Dust with rooting hormone, and bury that section of the stem 5–7.5cm (2–3in) deep in the improved soil. Hold firmly in place with two strong wire hoops, one each side of the cut, or with a large stone. Tie the shoot tip to a cane to train it vertically. Wait at least a year, until strong new growth is visible and the plant resists when tugged, indicating that it is well rooted. Then dig up and replant elsewhere.

AIR LAYERING

This technique is mainly used for hard-to-root house plants such as ficus. Instead of taking the stem down to the ground, place moist compost round a stem and hold it in place by binding thin polythene around it. Use the equivalent amount of compost to that held in a 10–15cm (4–6in) pot. Make a sloping cut through part of the stem, prop it open and treat with rooting powder, as for outdoor layering. With air layering, it is evident that the shoot has rooted when roots can be seen round the edge of the plastic. When this happens, cut through the stem just below the roots, and pot the young plant up. Air layering is sometimes recommended for outdoor shrubs but it is not really practical as the compost dries out too quickly and can heat up or freeze, according to the weather.

▷ STRAWBERRIES *produce runners that root naturally in soil. Peg them down into pots of compost and detach when well-rooted.*

Pruning tools

Pruning, trimming and training are not only essential to maintain a tidy garden, but are some of the most creative aspects of gardening, giving you an opportunity to control growth and determine the size, shape and habit of your shrubs. It is vital to have the correct tools for the job and to keep them sharp and in good condition. Secateurs are the basic pruning tool, but more specialized equipment is available for other cutting jobs round the garden.

△ BUY GARDEN SHEARS
of good quality and keep the blades clean and sharp so they will cut cleanly without tearing.

CHOOSING THE RIGHT PRUNING TOOLS

❖

Secateurs come in a range of sizes and weights, so try several before buying. If possible, use them to cut through branches to see if the handles fit your hand and that the spring is not too powerful for your grip. If too heavy, they will be tiring to work with for any length of time. Some secateurs are specially designed for left-handed use. Choose a model that is appropriate for the type of pruning your garden requires – there is no need to buy heavy-duty secateurs or loppers if you have only a few small trees. Buy the best quality you can afford, as good tools last longer and work better during their life.

SECATEURS
Secateurs are for pruning and cutting woody stems up to 1cm (½in) in diameter; they come in two distinct types. Bypass secateurs have two opposing blades, rather like heavy-duty scissors, which glide past each other; they are often thought to give more precision cutting. Anvil secateurs have a single blade that cuts against a flat plate, more like slicing down on to a board. This action can cause slight crushing or bruising of plant stems, which you would not want when taking woody cuttings for propagation, for instance. However, when old or slightly blunt, they give a cleaner cut than bypass secateurs in the same condition. A ratchet version of anvil secateurs makes cutting easier for people with weak or arthritic hands.

◁ A FOLDING PRUNING SAW (top) is *not much bigger than secateurs (anvil, above and bypass, left) but will deal with tree branches. Tools with bright handles are less easily lost when put down in the garden.*

LOPPERS
Long-handled, heavy-duty cutters are available in various styles for tough pruning of thick or out-of-reach branches. Long-handled loppers resemble croppers, but with secateur blades that will slice through branches 5cm (2in) or more in diameter. Some manufacturers supply long-handled extensions to which specially adapted secateurs and pruning saws can be fitted for tackling tall trees without having to use a ladder; the same handles can then be used with a fruit picking net.

SNIPS
Halfway between scissors and secateurs, snips are intended for lightweight jobs such as dead-heading and cutting flowers, as an alternative to picking them with your fingers. They are also handy for trimming and tidying plants on which it is inappropriate to use shears, perhaps for large-leaved topiary plants such as bay (*Laurus nobilis*), where shearing would cut some leaves in half. Flower gatherers are a variation of snips, where a secondary blade grasps the flower stem after cutting, preventing it from dropping to the ground.

◁ TRIMMED TREES *such as these potted standard bays make a good formal feature. Maintain their shape by pruning them lightly several times during the growing season.*

USING SECATEURS

○ Hold secateurs or loppers firmly in your hand with the larger blade uppermost, and position them at 90° to the stem you are cutting or, on plants with alternate growing buds, at a more sloping angle.

○ Use with a scissor action to produce the cleanest cut.

○ Do not twist the secateurs from side to side or tug at a tough stem, as this only tears the fibres of the stem, making it harder to cut through and damaging the plant.

○ Instead, bend the branch slightly downwards, away from the blades, to open the cut up a little, making it easier to slice through.

63

PRUNING SAW

These are special saws with narrow blades, good for getting in and out between closely spaced branches. Fairly coarse teeth make much lighter work of sawing green wood than a fine-toothed carpentry saw. Small, folding pruning saws are also available that fit into a pocket. Use a pruning saw for branches that are too thick to cut with secateurs; a saw can be used for material several centimetres thick as well as for cutting down saplings or small trees.

GARDEN SHEARS

Shears are used for various clipping jobs: trimming short lengths of hedge such as dwarf box edgings, for trimming topiary shapes, and for dead-heading shrubs like heathers and lavender after flowering. Two-handled hedging shears are the most convenient for general use, but sheep shears – which only need one hand – are handy for small areas of fine trimming and the dead-heading of dwarf flowering hedges.

▽ SINGLE-HANDED SHEARS *(shown here) or sheep shears are ideal for precision-trimming topiary like this box spiral.*

CARING FOR YOUR TOOLS

○ Wipe the blades with a damp cloth and a little washing-up liquid after use to remove sap, which makes the cutting surfaces sticky and prevents a good cut next time.

○ Leave secateurs with the blades open to dry thoroughly before putting them away.

○ Wipe blades over with an oily rag before prolonged storage, and keep in a dry environment to prevent rusting.

○ Some secateurs are dismantled for sharpening; others can be sharpened using a long, narrow sharpening stone. Sharpen regularly to avoid tearing the bark or damaging plant tissues.

▷ LONG-HANDLED LOPPERS *allow you extra purchase when cutting thick branches.*

Why prune?

Pruning is the gardening task that causes most worry to new gardeners, yet it is not complicated. Many plants in fact need little or no regular pruning, and even for those that do, minimal pruning often gives perfectly good results. A practical demonstration by another gardener is the best way to learn but you will not go far wrong if you follow the general guidelines given here.

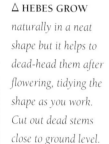

△ HEBES GROW *naturally in a neat shape but it helps to dead-head them after flowering, tidying the shape as you work. Cut out dead stems close to ground level.*

64

PRUNING SHRUBS

Any formative pruning needed to develop the shape of a plant (such as a standard tree or a bush shape) will have been done by the nursery before you buy and after that you simply need to prune only to retain this shape or in some cases to control the size of the shrub. As a general rule, shrubs that flower before early midsummer should be pruned immediately after flowering and those that flower later should be pruned in early spring, just before bud-burst.

▷ TO REJUVENATE AND CONTROL *an overgrown buddleja, cut it back by about one-third to a half in late summer, after flowering, then prune it down to about 1m (3ft) from the ground in mid-spring.*

• Remove dead, diseased or damaged shoots as soon as they are seen, to maintain the plant's health.
• Cut out any all-green ('reverted') shoots from variegated plants whenever they develop.
• Shorten over-long shoots and thin out congested or crossing stems to improve plant shape while plants are dormant, in winter or early spring.
• The plants that benefit most from annual pruning are vigorous spring-flowering shrubs such as philadelphus, forsythia and ribes: simply cut flowered stems back to their junction with a strong, young shoot. Modern bush roses need hard pruning every spring.

Shaping young plants

To form a dense, well-balanced shape, nip out the growing tip about 10cm (4in) above the top of the pot when potting up rooted cuttings. This is called 'stopping' and encourages the shoot to branch instead of growing straight up and making a leggy plant. When the side shoots are 5–7.5cm (2–3in) long, nip out their tips, giving them a second stopping. Use this technique when growing your own pelargoniums, fuchsias and bushy shrubs.

Rejuvenating old or out-of-shape plants

Some overgrown shrubs, such as rhododendrons, camellias and eucalyptus, respond well to being cut down to 30–60cm (1–2ft) above ground level in mid-spring; the resulting strong shoots are then thinned to make a bushy, well-shaped plant. Expect flowering plants rejuvenated in this way to miss a year or two's flowering. Most shrubs are

◁ THE MAJORITY *of popular garden shrubs need no regular pruning at all, except to tidy out-of-shape branches, control their size if necessary or remove any reverted stems from variegated cultivars.*

nip out their growing tips. Repeat several times as new side shoots appear to form a dense, bushy head above a clear stem. Use this technique for fuchsia, bay, rosemary, ribes and other suitable plants when grown in containers or in the open garden.

PRUNING CLIMBERS

Climbers allowed to ramble informally through trees rarely need pruning. When grown against walls or trellis, climbers such as honeysuckle and jasmine should have their main stems tied in to space them evenly over the area and create a framework. The side shoots from these stems will carry the flowers each year and their long growth is best pruned back, sufficiently to keep the plants tidy, in mid-spring. Rejuvenate top-heavy climbers that are bare at the base by cutting them down to 30cm (12in) above ground level in mid-spring; train the new growth out over the wall; do not expect any flowers the first year after such a radical prune. (The pruning of clematis, wisteria, hydrangea and roses is covered on the following pages.)

REASONS FOR PRUNING

❖

The aim of pruning is to help plants flower or fruit more productively and to control their shape and size. Without pruning, you will still get some flowers or fruit – plants simply do not achieve their full potential. Young plants also need pruning to form a well-shaped bush or tree initially. Mature plants may be pruned to reduce their size, improve their shape or to rejuvenate overgrown or neglected specimens. The removal of old wood encourages productive young growth and reducing the total branch area means that fruit or flowers on the remaining stems will be bigger. They may also be better coloured, since 'thinning' allows each branch to receive more light and air.

△ ONCE THE BASIC SHAPE *of a standard fuchsia has been formed, prune only to trim the 'head' to reduce it by two-thirds, after leaf-fall.*

better rejuvenated more gradually, by removing just one or two older branches (recognizable by their darker-coloured or craggier bark) just above ground level each year, in mid-spring.

Training a standard

Start with a rooted cutting and, instead of pinching out the growing tip as usual, tie it loosely to a cane pushed into the side of the pot. Remove all side shoots as the plant grows. When the stem reaches the required height, nip out the growing tip and allow three or five side shoots to grow out from immediately below it. When they are 5cm (2in) long,

Special pruning needs

Certain groups of deciduous flowering shrubs and climbers need regular pruning to improve their display and these include some of the most popular garden plants: roses, clematis, wisteria and hydrangea. Without pruning, the flowers of these plants may be lost among excess leafy growth or may be produced so high up that they can only be seen from an upstairs window. In pruning these plants, the aim is to control their size yet encourage free flowering.

△ **PRUNE HYBRID CLEMATIS** *in late winter/early spring, cutting all the stems off close to ground level. Also use this method to rejuvenate overgrown species of clematis, such as C. montana.*

66

PRUNING ROSES

If unpruned, roses become tall and woody and carry few flowers, mainly at the top of the plants, where they cannot be enjoyed.

• Prune **modern bush roses** in mid-spring, after the worst frosts are over. Cut plants back to 30–45cm (12–18in) above ground level, pruning strong stems back least and weak ones most to even out growth (hard-pruned stems grow away strongest).

• Prune **shrub roses** and old-fashioned roses after flowering, by removing the dead flowerheads plus about 20cm (8in) of stem.

• Do not prune **shrub roses** that have good hips as this will stop them being produced.

• Prune **climbing roses** when all their flowering is finished (some varieties flower twice in summer, others only once), cutting back side shoots to within 8–10cm (3–4in) of the main framework of branches tied out over the wall.

• Shorten the main branches of **climbers** to keep them within their allotted area.

• Prune **ramblers** after blooming to cut flowered stems back to their junction with a strong, new shoot. This will produce replacement stems that will carry next year's flowers.

• Remove all weak, diseased, damaged or congested stems entirely.

PRUNING CLEMATIS

If unpruned, clematis eventually grow big and tangled, with bare bases to their stems; the flowers of some

◁ **CLIMBING AND RAMBLER ROSES** *look superb trained over a pergola. Annual pruning keeps them free-flowering and vigorous.*

▷ **WISTERIA AND CLEMATIS** *produce prolific flowering displays when correctly pruned; if left, they can be disappointing and even, in the case of wisteria, a nuisance.*

varieties grow so high up they cannot be enjoyed. Since clematis vary in pruning needs from one variety to another, always keep the nursery label as this includes pruning instructions, or copy them on to the back of the plant label for easy reference. If you do not have the nursery label, consult a specialist guide book before pruning to ensure you prune each type correctly.

• Prune hybrid clematis varieties that flower at the tips of their shoots (these flower in mid- to late summer) in late winter or very early spring: cut them down to a pair of new buds close to ground level.

• Other hybrid varieties, which flower on short side shoots grown in the current year, are best left unpruned (these are varieties that start flowering in early summer). If overgrown, cut back hard in early spring; they will still flower but at a later time.

• Clematis species, such as *C. montana*, do not normally need pruning; if overgrown, cut them back hard in early spring and train the new stems into place.

PRUNING WISTERIA

Left unpruned, wisterias will grow into enormous, straggling vines, choked with vigorous twining stems produced at the expense of flowers.

• Start by training a framework of main stems out over the area to be covered and tie in place.

• Each year, in midsummer, cut back the new shoots growing from the main branches (these are green, as against the

brown skin of older shoots) to about 15–20cm (6–8in) from the main stems.

• In midwinter, go over plants again and shorten to about 2.5cm (1in) the side shoots that grew from these stubs at the end of the summer. This encourages the formation of twiggy 'spurs', from which the flowers grow.

PRUNING HYDRANGEAS

Do not dead-head these shrubs after flowering; if the dead flowerheads are left on all winter they act as umbrellas, sheltering the young shoots beneath them from severe weather.

• Prune hydrangeas in mid-spring, cutting them off just above a young shoot to remove dead flowerheads plus a few centimetres of stem.

• Do not prune mophead or lacecap hydrangeas too hard, or cut off shoots with a fat green bud at the tip, as these are the stems that will flower in the current year.

• Varieties of *Hydrangea paniculata*, however, can be pruned hard to encourage shoots to grow from the base.

▷ **RESIST THE** *temptation to dead-head your hydrangeas after flowering or prune too hard in spring: both will spoil next year's flowering.*

THE CORRECT CUT

○ Use sharp secateurs to make a clean cut and always cut just above a leaf joint or growth bud, as the next young shoot will grow out from here.

○ On plants such as roses, that have alternate growth buds, make an angled cut, sloping it slightly away from the bud side of the shoot.

○ Prune above a bud that is pointing in the direction in which you want the new shoot to grow. Cut to outward-facing buds to make a dense bush grow more open in habit; and cut to an upward-facing bud to make a droopy plant grow more strongly upright.

○ On plants that have opposite buds, like hydrangea, make a straight cut just above a strong pair of buds or shoots, taking care not to damage them. If you want to encourage growth in one direction only, remove the unwanted bud or shoot after making the cut.

○ Delay pruning for a few weeks if cold weather persists in spring, as pruning encourages the production of vigorous new shoots whose growth is very soft and can be killed by late frost.

○ When clematis, wisteria or climbing roses are grown informally, rambling through trees, no pruning is necessary.

67

Dealing with pests and diseases

Vine weevil

A garden is a haven for a wide variety of insect life, much of which is a great asset to the gardener. Only a small number of species are harmful to plants and where chemicals are not used indiscriminately these will be controlled naturally by beneficial predators. To reduce the risk of attack by pests and diseases, buy healthy plants and practise good garden hygiene. If it becomes necessary to use chemical insecticides or chemical forms of disease control, treat only affected plants and take precautions to avoid harming beneficial creatures such as bees.

IDENTIFYING GARDEN PESTS

A huge range of insect and other pests can attack plants in the garden, making ornamental plants unsightly and edible crops less palatable. Pests can also threaten the lives of plants by weakening them or by spreading viral disease. Since it is much easier to keep plants free from pests than to nurse them back to health after serious damage has been done, it is worth learning to recognize the most common enemies and check for them regularly.

Described below are the insects and other pests that regularly attack garden plants. The various methods of control are explained in more detail on the following pages.

Greenfly (aphids) are small, wingless insects found on the tips of shoots and buds and the undersides of leaves, both outdoors and in the greenhouse; the name greenfly is misleading as aphids can also be pink, cream or brown. Control by hand by washing aphids off leaves or tips, or spray with selective aphicide. Many natural predators control aphids, including lacewings, ladybirds, hoverfly and blue tits.

Vine weevil adults are brown beetles 1cm (⅜in) in length whose long snouts bite scalloped notches round the edges of evergreen leaves such as rhododendron; their larvae are fat, white, C-shaped grubs that live in soil, feeding on the roots of cyclamen, primulas and other plants, both in pots and in borders. Control by hand or use biological control nematodes.

Brassica whitefly are like tiny white insects; they resemble the glasshouse whitefly but live outdoors on brassica

crops like cabbages as well as on weeds of the same family. They are fairly resistant to chemical sprays, so the best remedy is to cover plants with fleece.

Slugs are a familiar, slimy pest that rasp soft tissues from plants, leaving characteristic lacy holes. Offenders can often be caught red-handed by torch-light at night, but on bright days they hide away in cool, dark places to avoid drying up. The most effective, though expensive, remedy is biological control in the form of nematodes. Water on to the soil over whole borders during the warmer months, especially round plants most at risk, such as hostas. Use slug pellets sparingly and hide them under broken pots to protect pets and birds.

Snails cause similar damage to that of slugs but will climb woody stems and walls to reach soft plant material, making nematodes ineffective; hunt out groups hibernating in wall-niches in winter and destroy, or use pellets with care.

◁ **ALL GREENFLY** *are females and produce live young, ready to feed immediately – and within a few days the young greenfly can also lay young.*

Woodlice

Lily beetle

Woodlice are grey creatures 5mm (⅕in) long that roll up into balls when disturbed. They feed on decaying vegetation and as such are beneficial to compost heaps. They may, however, take weak seedlings or attack plants already damaged by other causes, especially in greenhouses. Good hygiene, keeping the garden free from dead vegetation and debris, is the best remedy.

Earwigs are slender creatures, 2.5cm (1in) long, with a pair of pincers at the rear end. They bite holes in flower petals, especially of exhibition-type blooms such as dahlia and chrysanthemum. Good garden hygiene is the best remedy or you could make old-fashioned earwig traps, placing upturned plant pots stuffed with scrunched-up newspaper on top of canes among plants. Empty daily and destroy pests. Earwigs do some good in the garden by feeding on greenfly.

Millipedes are slow-moving, black, pencil-shaped creatures with many legs moving in 'waves' along the body; they feed on plants. Avoid introducing them to the garden by checking new plants for passengers and physically remove any you see.

Lily beetles are small, bright red beetles infesting lilies and related plants; the larvae resemble dark, slimy bird droppings and eat foliage. They are a relatively new pest in warmer areas. Physical removal is the best remedy; chemicals are not very effective against them.

Leaf miners are small, cream torpedo-shaped larvae that tunnel inside leaves, creating wiggly white tunnels between the upper and lower surfaces of leaves. Pick off affected leaves by hand. Spraying systemic insecticide may help deter adults laying eggs if done early in the season.

Codling moth larvae are the maggots inside apples. As an alternative to regular preventative spraying, codling moth traps may be hung in fruit trees in early summer, using one for every five or six trees – these lure adult male codling moths to sticky paper by using pheromone scent, killing the males and preventing the females being fertilized and laying eggs.

GREENHOUSE PESTS

Red spider mites are minute, light brown or orange, dust-like insects causing a mottled appearance to leaves. Fine webbing may be evident. High humidity deters them, so damp down greenhouses by spraying paths with water on warm days. Alternatively, use pesticide sprays or introduce the predatory mite *Phytoseiulus* to control them naturally.

Whitefly, which resemble tiny white moths, can be found on the undersides of greenhouse plants, taking to the air in white clouds when disturbed. Control by regular chemical sprays or introduce the predatory, parasitic wasp, *Encarsia formosa.* Avoid overcrowding plants and ventilate the greenhouse well.

Thrips are minute flies whose larvae live inside plants and cause tiny silvery speckles on foliage. Use dilute systemic insecticide, drenching compost and spraying plants with the solution.

◁ HOLD A LEAF *up to the light to locate a leaf miner; squeeze the larva between your fingers to kill it.*

69

Sciarid (mushroom fly) are tiny black flies hovering round compost heaps and pots of plants (especially those growing in peat-based compost); their larvae are tiny white 'worms' in the compost. Springtails are similar but their larvae jump when pots are watered. To control, drench compost with spray-strength systemic insecticide.

PEST CONTROL TECHNIQUES

Various methods, both natural and biological, can be used to control pests though it is always preferable to prevent any infestations in the first place by buying healthy plants and practising good garden hygiene. Chemical pesticides are useful as a last resort, although nowadays there are plenty of 'green' alternatives.

△ **USE STICKY TRAPS** *in the greenhouse to snare pests like whitefly; for best results, suspend just above favourite plants like fuchsias and disturb plants occasionally to set insects flying.*

Manual forms of control

Some pests can be kept at bay by hand, without resorting to using insecticides, and this should always be the first means to try. Slow-moving, non-flying insects like aphids are easily wiped off the leaves and tips of shoots, for example. Individual caterpillars may be picked off plants by hand and you can make old-fashioned slug traps by sinking saucers of beer in among plants. In the kitchen garden you can pinch out the tips of broad beans to deter blackfly and prune out the webs of tent-forming caterpillars from fruit trees.

Using natural predators

It is vital to know which the natural predators of various plant pests are, to avoid destroying them by mistake.

Natural predators include insectivorous birds like blue tits as well as shrews, frogs and toads, carnivorous beetles, centipedes, spiders and hoverfly and lacewing larvae. Both the larvae and adults of some flying insects, like ladybirds, feed on greenfly, and several wasp species parasitize plant pests such as caterpillars by laying their eggs inside the body; the larvae then destroy the pest. To encourage natural predators into the garden, first stop using chemicals; you could also make a pond and leave plant debris round the edge of the garden to protect spiders in winter.

Biological control

Many common pests can now be controlled by using specially introduced predators and parasitic insects. The secret of their success is

to use them at the right time. Under glass, use *Phytoseiulus* (a predatory mite) to tackle red spider mite and *Encarsia formosa* (a small wasp that parasitizes whitefly) in spring: a warm greenhouse is vital. These predators are supplied by post and released immediately to control infestations.

Two kinds of microscopic nematode (beneficial eelworms) are available to tackle slugs and vine weevils. Both kinds are mixed with water and applied via a fine rose on a watering can to the open soil around plants, to greenhouse border soil or, for vine weevil, to individual pots of plants at risk of attack, such as cyclamen or primulas. Use in spring when the temperature of the soil has risen above 10°C (50°F), and

70

PHYSICAL BARRIERS

❖

Barriers are mainly used to protect fruit and vegetables from pest attack; the barrier can take a variety of forms.

- Susceptible plants such as brassicas or rows of carrots may be covered with a very fine mesh net through their growing life to prevent insects from reaching them; the mesh is supported by hoops of wire, tied loosely round individual plants, or laid over rows and dug into shallow trenches along the edges.

- Netting is often used to cover fruit cages to stop birds picking the fruit

and similar structures can be used to screen vegetable plots from pigeons or butterflies.

- Grease bands are sometimes put around the trunks of fruit trees in winter to protect them from crawling pests. Pest-control 'glue' may be applied round the rim of tubs to deter slugs and snails.

- Fitting a collar (cardboard disc) snugly round the base of brassica stems will prevent the female cabbage root fly from reaching the soil to lay her eggs.

---

ensure that the soil is moist. Beneficial nematodes are unlikely to survive the winter outside in the garden, and even under glass they usually die out due to the interruption in their food supply, so it becomes neccesary to reapply them every year.

Using chemicals

Where there is no alternative to spraying with chemicals, choose products that control only the target pest, for instance selective aphicides that kill greenfly and blackfly without harming beneficial insects or bees that also feed on the plant. Check the manufacturer's label carefully. Most pesticides in fact kill a wide range of pests, so use them in the late evening, after bees have left the garden. Spray on a windless day and wear protective clothing such as gloves and goggles. Avoid spraying open flowers, or plants that are either under stress due to lack of water or suffering from disease.

For small gardens and occasional use, buy ready-mixed chemical products in

their own sprayer-bottles and use just what you need each time. This works out much more cheaply than buying concentrated products for which you need a separate sprayer and have to make up larger quantities than you need, wasting the rest.

Do not dispose of unwanted 'neat' chemicals down the drains – contact your local council for advice on where to put them. If you have small amounts of diluted chemicals left over after spraying, dispose of them by watering them down further and spraying the solution over vacant ground. Rinse out the sprayer after use and dispose of the rinsings over empty ground, in the same way.

Powdery mildew

Grey mould

DISEASE IN GARDEN PLANTS

Plant diseases due to fungus, bacteria or virus cause a wide range of different symptoms and can severely check the growth of mature plants or kill young ones. Garden hygiene and good cultural practices are the best ways to prevent disease but there are several means of control to tackle the various problems caused by disease.

Common diseases

A great number of different diseases can attack plants, though relatively few are common in gardens. Some affect only particular plants. The diseases described below are those most likely to be seen in gardens from time to time; the majority are easily prevented or controlled, often without resorting to chemicals.

Powdery mildew resembles a floury residue on the upper surfaces of plant leaves or stems, especially of roses and vines, in late summer. It usually occurs when plants are short of water: irrigate thoroughly during dry spells to help prevent it. To treat, spray with an appropriate fungicide.

Grey mould (botrytis) shows as fluffy, grey, mouldy patches on leaves, stems or dead flowerheads, usually on dead tissue or following an injury. Since it is encouraged by high humidity, ventilate the greenhouse regularly; good garden hygiene also helps to reduce its incidence. Spray with an appropriate fungicide.

Black spot is seen on rose foliage in the form of round black patches, which may spread until the leaves are almost covered; it can lead to premature leaf drop. Some rose varieties have a natural resistance, so grow these if you want to avoid spraying. Otherwise, spraying every two weeks with a suitable fungicide through the growing season is the only means of prevention. Gather and burn fallen leaves in autumn and spray bare stems and the soil beneath plants with a winter wash.

Black spot

72

Rust causes rusty orange or reddish pustules on leaves, particularly those of roses, pelargonium and leeks. Remove affected leaves if the infestation is light and spray regularly with a suitable fungicide to prevent outbreaks getting worse. Combined rose fungicides against rust, mildew and black spot often include an aphid killer too. Burn badly affected plants.

Rust on rose foliage

Honey fungus affects mainly woody plants, including hedges, which can die suddenly or sicken and die more gradually. The disease is mainly spread between plants by black 'bootlaces', which are sometimes found under the bark or in the soil, and in autumn golden toadstools may appear round the plant. In areas where honey fungus is prevalent, have dead tree stumps winched out so they cannot act as a source of infection. When planting into infected soil, surround new plants with a 60-cm (2-ft) deep polythene collar sunk into the ground round them to prevent infection by bootlaces.

Root rots cause the roots or necks of plants to rot away. Early symptoms include sudden wilting, followed by the rapid death of the plant, or reddish tints to the foliage of heathers and conifers, which fail gradually over time. Root rots are worst where the soil is poorly drained. Prevent harmful soil organisms building up to problem levels by not planting the same type of plant in the same place for successive years; use a crop rotation system on vegetable plots.

Damping off causes seedlings to collapse, as though their stems have been bent over close to the base, and rapidly die. It may be due to various cultural problems, such as unclean seed trays, propagator or growing medium, or can be caused by overcrowding or growing conditions that are too

cold or dark. Watering with a suitable fungicide may help but improving the growing conditions is the best solution.

Clematis wilt affects newly planted clematis, whose stems and leaves suddenly wilt, then turn brown as if scorched. If the affected stems are cut away, new growth often resprouts from the base, provided the clematis was originally planted deeply, with the rootball 10–15cm (4–6in) below the surface of the soil. Varieties of *Clematis viticella* appear immune.

Virus diseases cause a range of symptoms, most commonly mottled or streaked leaves and in some cases streaked flower colour. Affected plants grow poorly and the yields of vegetable plants or fruit bushes and canes are gradually reduced. Viruses are mainly transmitted between plants by aphids or other sap-sucking insects, so control these pests to limit the spread of viruses. Even virus-free plants are eventually affected, due to transmission by insects or on hands but they give good yields for some years before this happens. There is no cure; affected plants must be destroyed.

Physiological disorders

A huge range of strange symptoms that appear in plants, such as 'blind' shoots, blotchy fruit and discoloured leaves, are due to physical causes rather than insect infestation or disease. Extreme conditions such as drought or waterlogged soil, excessively high or low temperatures or humidity, and poor light or sun-scorch are common causes. Hail, wind, frost, scorching sun and weedkiller can also cause physical symptoms. The damage suffered cannot be reversed but new

◁ **HONEY FUNGUS** *affects shrubs and hedges and is spread below the bark. It may manifest itself in autumn as yellow toadstools round the base of the plant.*

conditions and much more likely that plants grow poorly and look sick due to shortage of a whole range of nutrients. This happens on impoverished soil when plants are not fed regularly, especially on soil with a very high or low pH, where nutrients are chemically 'locked up'. The solution is to remedy the growing conditions.

DISEASE CONTROL

As with pest control, various measures can be adopted, escalating in their seriousness from manual to chemical forms.

growth generally returns to normal once growing conditions are improved. Prune out damaged stems to improve the plant's appearance.

Nutritional disorders

Deficiency symptoms vary according to which elements are in short supply. With a nitrogen shortage, plant leaves are typically pale green and slightly stunted, with red or orange glints. Plants suffering from phosphate deficiency have bluish leaves with purplish or bronzy tints. A shortage of potash shows up as brown edges or brown spots on leaves. Chlorosis, caused by lack of iron, makes the leaves look yellow; this is a common problem, most often seen on lime-hating plants grown on chalky soil. It is unusual for a single nutrient to be deficient in garden

Manual forms of control

Check your plants regularly so problems can be detected early. If disease affects only a few leaves, pick them off by hand and burn to prevent spores spreading the disease. Make it a habit to remove dead leaves and flowerheads, and prune out dead stems or tips of shoots when you see them, as these are the first sites that disease organisms will invade. Protect plants from physical bruising or breakage as damaged tissues are susceptible to being infected by disease.

Cultural control

Meticulous garden hygiene, ensuring freedom from debris and weeds, and good growing conditions make for strong, healthy plants that are better able to withstand disease than weak specimens. In vegetable plots, practise

- Keep aphids under control because sap-sucking insects spread viral disease between plants in their saliva. Cover fruit bushes and vegetable crops with fine nets as an alternative to spraying.

- Use a garden disinfectant product to clean pots, seed trays and other propagation implements to reduce the risk of spreading disease.

- Buy seed and potting composts in quantities that can be used up quickly; re-seal the neck of the bag between uses to exclude airborne disease organisms.

- Clean knife or secateur blades with bleach or disinfectant from time to time when either propagating or pruning plants.

- Burn badly diseased plants to prevent organisms spreading; never put diseased material on to the compost heap or use diseased plants for propagation.

73

crop rotation to prevent a build-up of root disease in the soil. Check new plants for tell-tale disease symptoms and reject any unhealthy ones.

Chemical control

Regard spraying with chemicals as a last resort. It is effective mainly against fungal disease; few products tackle bacterial diseases and none treat viruses. Most fungicides work against several different fungal diseases so you need not identify the precise problem; read the label first, however. Follow the guidelines given for insecticides in the Safe Use of Chemicals box on the page 70.

Weeds and weeding

A weed is any plant growing in the wrong place and usually weeds are rampant species of wildflower that invade gardens by wind-borne seed, animal or bird vectors, or through roots or seed in manure. Invasive garden plants can themselves become weeds, due to excess seeding or spreading roots. The secret of a weed-free garden is never to let weeds get out of control: there are techniques for tackling even the most stubborn species.

IDENTIFYING COMMON WEEDS

Most common weeds, like groundsel and nettles, are well known to gardeners, but anything out of the ordinary can usually be identified by looking it up in a book of wildflowers. Otherwise, take a specimen to a garden centre or horticultural society to be looked at by someone more expert.

Annual weeds

Annual weeds are those, like groundsel, that flower, set seed and die in one year but others, such as bitter cress, produce several generations of seed each year. Neglected ground contains thousands of dormant weed seeds and when soil is cultivated they are brought to the surface and exposed to light, enabling them to germinate. Control by regular hoeing, hand weeding, mulching or use of contact weedkillers before flowering, so they cannot set seed.

Perennial weeds

Perennial weeds such as nettles and ground elder behave like herbaceous plants, dying down in autumn and reappearing the following spring. Small clumps may be dug up, but well-established colonies, especially of spreading perennials like couch grass and bindweed, are best treated with translocated weedkiller. When growing among cultivated plants, 'spot treat' individual weeds by spraying or painting with weedkiller. Regular hoeing also works, given time, by frequently cutting off new growth, eventually weakening the plant.

Woody weeds

Woody weeds like sycamore seedlings and brambles grow fast and are hard to dig out, on account of their deep roots. Dig out seedlings while young but cut off well-established plants close to ground level and treat the resulting vigorous new growth with brushwood killer. Protect nearby plants.

COMMON PROBLEM WEEDS

Bindweed, a vigorous, twining plant with large, white, trumpet-shaped flowers, spreads by thick, white, brittle underground roots – new plants are readily propagated if these are broken by digging. When plants first emerge above ground in spring they form a rosette before climbing: treat at this stage with translocated weedkiller and repeat when regrowth appears. Cut off scrambling stems among shrubs at ground level: leave the stems to die, after which they are easier to untangle. Treat new growth at ground level as it emerges.

Couch grass is a wiry grass that spreads by thin white underground rhizomes. Small clumps may be dug out but all root must be removed. Spray larger areas with translocated weedkiller and wait until the foliage turns brown before removing debris, to ensure the roots are dead. Clear heavily infested sites by covering whole areas with thick black polythene or old carpet to cut out light. Leave in place for at least a year.

Creeping buttercup   *Horsetail*

△ BINDWEED *has deceptively pretty white trumpet flowers but if left unchecked it soon spreads to form a dense cover that will smother cultivated plants, such as this artichoke.*

Creeping buttercup is a low, spreading, rosette-like buttercup with plantlets at the ends of runner-like stems (like strawberry runners). It has a tough root system from which the top of the plant snaps off when pulled but the remains regenerate quickly. Spot-treat rosettes with weedkiller and prevent runners rooting by early weeding. Never put on the compost heap.

Celandine is a pretty spring wildflower with yellow, buttercup-like blooms and low rosettes of deep green foliage. Plants die down in early summer, leaving clusters of tiny, fragile bulbils underground. Digging breaks up clusters and distributes bulbils even more widely through the soil – they are too small to remove by hand. Water

foliage with contact weedkiller before flowering. One treatment will usually be effective.

Ground elder has short, upright growth with characteristic elder-bush type foliage and flat white heads of flowers; it spreads by strong underground stems and roots. Digging is ineffective as broken root fragments propagate new plants. Spray young growth with translocated weedkiller in spring and retreat each time new shoots appear. Or grass over the area and cut regularly to prevent regrowth. It may take several years to eradicate strong colonies.

Horsetail is a primitive plant related to the fossilized remains of the giant horsetail, found in coal seams; new

growth resembles asparagus tips from which tall, ferny foliage develops later. The roots can penetrate huge distances. Do not try to dig out as damaged roots regrow. Weedkillers are not very effective against horsetail, so mow it out of lawns, hoe borders regularly to weaken it, use path weedkiller on gravel or paving and try systemic herbicides on vacant land or among shrubs.

Wild ivy can damage loose mortar in walls and unstable fences with its penetrating aerial roots and smother shrubs and hedges with its shoots. If large quantities build up in the heads of old trees, this can increase their wind resistance enough to bring them down on stormy nights. Remove ivy seedlings while young and pull out climbing stems from the base of hedges regularly. To remove established ivy from trees, cut through the base of stems near ground level; when the foliage turns brown, the stems are easier to strip off. Ivy stumps can be treated with brushwood killer to prevent regrowth. Though not a parasite on other plants, ivy uses them for support as it climbs and can smother small plants.

75

Ground elder

USING WEEDKILLER SAFELY

❖

- Apply most weedkillers in mid-spring to early summer, when weeds are young and growing rapidly, before they start flowering.

- Apply translocated and contact weedkillers to foliage, not soil. Do not apply liquid kinds when rain is expected or the product will be washed off before it is absorbed.

- Keep weedkiller off plants you wish to retain; in a border, shield plants with plastic or cardboard while treating weeds using a coarse rose on a watering can, or treat weeds individually using weedkiller gel or a ready-mixed spray sold in a spray-bottle.

- Have a separate watering can and sprayer specially for weedkillers, and label it clearly to avoid mistakes.

- Read the manufacturer's instructions carefully before using weedkillers, and follow them to the letter.

- Do not use weedkillers on windy days as vapour droplets can 'drift' on to nearby beds.

- Keep bottles and packets of weedkiller in a safe place, where pets and children cannot reach them. When empty, dispose of them carefully.

WEED CONTROL TECHNIQUES

Weeds can be controlled by manual means, such as hand-weeding or hoeing, by physical methods such as smothering under a mulch, or by using chemical weedkillers. Well-established weeds may need several treatments or, in some cases, prolonged persistence to eradicate them. New weeds constantly find their way into the garden from seeds that are accidentally introduced with new plants or bought-in manure, as well as being dropped by birds or borne on the wind.

The right weedkiller

There are several kinds of weedkiller, so make sure you select an appropriate type for the job in hand.

Contact weedkillers are best used on annual weeds and work directly on the foliage. Treated weeds look 'scorched' within a few days.

Translocated weedkillers are intended for perennial weeds. They are taken in by the leaves and move through the plant, taking several weeks to kill it, root and all. Established clumps may need several treatments.

Brushwood killers suit tougher weeds with woody stems as well as saplings and tree stumps. Use with care.

Path weedkillers are residual, so use them only on gravel drives and cracks between paving, not in plant borders. Best applied in mid- to late spring, they will prevent weeds growing for the rest of the season.

Preventing weeds

Check before buying to make sure you are not bringing home weeds with your new plants, since a lot of problem weeds like bitter cress are accidentally 'bought in' with plants. Always scrape off and discard the mossy and weedy surface layer on the compost of purchased plants.

For a permanently weed-free garden, cover the ground with plastic or a landscape fabric, insert plants in crosses cut in the material, then spread gravel or bark chippings on top to hide the plastic.

Mulching

Spread a 5–10cm (2–4in) layer of well-rotted manure or compost over the soil to suppress weeds by keeping germinated weed seeds in the dark. Or cover with a 2.5–5cm (1–2in) layer of inorganic material like gravel or with cocoa shells or wood chippings. Mulching has little effect on established perennial weeds as they can push up through an organic mulch (but not a plastic one).

Hand-weeding

Use a hand fork to weed between small plants on a rockery or in crowded borders where there is no room to hoe. An old dinner fork is useful for teasing out weeds in cracks between paving (*see left*).

A hoe, which has a sharp blade, can be pushed or pulled through the soil surface to cut off weeds at the root. To make light of the job, hoe while weeds are still tiny; barely moving the soil surface is enough to uproot newly germinated weed

◁ COARSE BARK CHIPPINGS *make a long-lasting surface mulch material: use in a deep layer between trees and shrubs for a natural-looking and very practical soil topping.*

seedlings, which quickly wither away – there is no need to clear up afterwards. 'Chop' larger weeds out with a hoe, then rake up.

Barriers

Create a weed barrier by spreading sheets of black plastic, old carpet or heavy-duty landscape fabric over the soil; these are strong enough to keep perennial weeds covered and eventually they die from lack of light. After two years, even problem weeds can be eradicated. A vertical barrier, such as thick black plastic sunk 60cm (2ft) or more into the soil, is an effective way to prevent problem weeds spreading under a fence or hedge from adjacent land, or to contain patches of problem weeds.

WEED CONTROL TOOLS

DRAW HOE: for hoeing between straight rows of vegetables, but also useful for 'hooking' weeds out from borders.

DUTCH HOE: best used frequently when weeds are barely visible, to help keep the soil weed-free.

BORDER OR DIGGING FORK: for digging out clumps of perennial weeds.

HAND FORK OR TROWEL: for light hand-weeding between plants.

Push or Dutch hoe

Draw hoe

CLEARING VACANT GROUND

- Use a flame gun to kill existing annual weeds and the tops of perennial weeds. This encourages dormant seed to germinate fast, so re-treat when new growth appears.

- Water or spray translocated weedkiller over the entire area; two or more treatments may be needed for mature perennial weeds.

- Cover the entire area with black plastic, old carpet or similar and leave it in place for up to two years to smother out perennial or problem weeds.

- Regular mowing will get rid of any upright weeds in time, but not grassy, creeping or rosette types. Try sowing a weedy area with grass seed and cut weekly. It will take two to three years to eradicate the weeds fully, then you can kill off the grass and cultivate the area.

∇ MULCHES AND BARRIERS
Use organic mulches alone over bare soil, or use them over a permanent inorganic barrier for a garden that stays totally weed-free.

Non-porous ground matting

Cocoa shell mulch

Porous ground matting

Bark mulch